monday morning®

FABULOUS FRIENDS

And Other Storybook Themes

by Maxine Riggers
illustrated by Marilynn G. Barr
cover art by Terrence Meagher

Publisher: Roberta Suid
Copy Editor: Carol Whiteley
Design and Production: Susan Pinkerton

Maxine Riggers is a former kindergarten teacher who has been telling stories at libraries and schools for over 12 years. She is the author of *Amazing Alligators and Other Story Hour Friends*, and has instructed librarians on how to hold successful story hours.

Unless otherwise noted, Maxine Riggers is the author of all poems, songs, and finger plays.

12.95

CONTENTS

INTRODUCTION 4

PROGRAMS

Beautiful Bugs 5

Colorful Clothes 25

Fabulous Friends 47

Frivolous Food 67

Grand Grandparents 83

Happy Homes 103

RESOURCES 123

INDEX 125

INTRODUCTION

Storytellers, teachers, librarians, and parents—this book will help you present storybooks in a fun and meaningful way. The six chapters in FABULOUS FRIENDS cover topics that interest children: bugs, clothes, food, friends, grandparents, and homes—and the theme-units provide a multitude of ideas for extending the reading experience. Each of the chapters focuses on eight books especially suited for read-alouds, with accompanying projects to extend the stories. Another 30 to 50 books are included in the "More Books" section of each chapter, with a synopsis of each book; these books make good lap books, but can also be used for read-alouds. Each chapter also includes poems, songs, finger plays, games, crafts, and snacks.

Make Reading Fun

Libraries have been transformed from places where children were advised to "hush" to lively environments filled with fun, stimulating activities, including summer reading programs, year-around story hours, singing, game playing, and story dramatizations. These kinds of activities entice children into the library, and instill in them an interest in reading. This early love of reading will stay with them as they get older, and they'll continue to use and enjoy the library.

Don't be afraid to try new activities with your students. Remember, today's educators are competing with videos and other media, and it's our responsibility to see that books are given a chance. This book is filled with ideas for developing such activities.

Use Props in Storytelling

The use of props is important in storytelling—props provide something tangible for children to see, have, or hold that are a part of the story. Props may also help tell a story or be an extension of a story, for instance, each child can have a spider just like the one in THE VERY BUSY CATERPILLAR by Eric Carle.

Props also provide a visual experience that helps children retain a story in their mind. For example, "fake" food hanging from the ceiling could be a reminder of CLOUDY WITH A CHANCE OF MEATBALLS by Judy Barrett. And taking apart a nesting doll when reading THE WOODEN DOLL by Susan Bonners could help the children understand the idea more clearly.

Use the Flannel Board to Develop Creativity

Flannel board stories are an excellent way to interest children in books. As you read a book, place felt pieces at the appropriate time on the flannel board. Let the children assist you in putting up the pieces on cue. Later, make the book and felt pieces readily available for the children to use when retelling the story or making up their own. Children who are reluctant to participate in dramatic play often find satisfaction in retelling a story using the flannel board.

Most stories can be told on the flannel board, but for young children it's best to choose stories that have a sequence, a simple plot, and simple characters. Felt pieces are easy to make by copying the outline of illustrations onto different colors of felt and cutting them out. These pieces can be placed on the flannel board in either direction to direct the flow of the story. Or you can copy illustrations onto paper, then color, cut out, and laminate them and glue flannel scraps onto the backs.

Bugs are creepy, crawly critters! But you can find them in some fabulous "buggy" stories (as well as under rocks). Plan to tell stories about bugs during the warm months when the children can go on a bug observation walk.

Before beginning a unit on bugs, read BUGS by Nancy Winslow Parker. This helpful resource provides general information about a variety of bugs. Also form a "Bugs for Books Club" to encourage children to read books on bugs. Each child should set his or her own goal as to how many books to read. Give the children a "Bugs for Books Club" certificate when they have reached their goal. (See the certificate provided.) The certificates may be displayed on the wall or sent home to parents.

Declare a special day to be "National Bug Day." Have the children do a variety of buggy things on that day. Invite a specialist in your area to "show and tell" about bugs. Or watch a bug video together.

Hold an "Eric Carle Day." Display all of Eric Carle's books about bugs along with a picture of him. Talk about his accomplishments as an author and read only his books that day.

SETTING THE STAGE

Use bug puppets as much as possible to liven up the room and to create interest in stories about bugs. Ladybug, firefly, grasshopper, and spider puppets may be purchased from Folkmanis Inc. (see Resources). Several bug hand puppet patterns are available from Butterick Pattern Co. Use the illustration "Be a Bookworm!" as a guideline to create a huge (eight- to ten-foot-long) bookworm as a wall or hall display. Have the children help

decorate it. Encourage the children to make the bookworm very colorful to attract lots of attention.

Place an ant colony in the room and set various ant books nearby to create an interest in ant stories.

Put out several "magic carpets" (carpet or fabric pieces), and let the children fly to Bugsville. Have the children make different bug sounds to locate the town—cricket chirps, fly buzzing, and bee humming.

BULLETIN BOARD IDEAS

1. Use an opaque projector to enlarge and copy the "Books Are Bugwonderful" illustration onto poster paper. Color and mat the illustration before pinning it up. For an even greater effect, make the poster three dimensional by cutting out the lettering and the bug's head and gluing them onto the paper. Add yarn for hair, pipe cleaners for antennae, and pompons for eyes.

2. Enlarge an outline of the "very hungry caterpillar" onto poster paper. Cut shades of green and yellow art tissue paper into small pieces and glue them onto the caterpillar. Glue on red tissue pieces for the head and purple for the antennae. Do the same thing to make the butterfly from the story's finale, but use a variety of colors.

3. Title the bulletin board "Aranea" (a book by Jenny Wagner) or the title of any other book about spiders. Follow the directions in the Bug Crafts section to make spiders and a huge spider web big enough to cover the entire bulletin board.

Bugs for Books Club

_____ has read _____

Name   No.

of Bug Books and is an official member of the
Bugs for Books Club.

_____

Signature

ANANSI AND THE MOSS-COVERED ROCK
retold by Eric A. Kimmel, il. by Janet Stevens (Holiday House, 1988).

Story: Anansi, the legendary spider, uses a strange moss-covered rock found in the forest to trick a lion, an elephant, a rhinoceros, a hippopotamus, a giraffe, and many other animals. Finally, little Bush Deer teaches Anansi a lesson.

Materials: moss-covered rock, spider puppet (see Bug Crafts)

Directions: Introduce this story by showing a real moss-covered rock. (If you can't find one, make one by gluing moss—found in floral or variety shops—onto any rock.) Ask why the children think this rock might be unique. Introduce the spider puppet and make him collapse every time he comes close to the rock; the children will delight in seeing this. Ask the children to join in on the refrain "Isn't this a strange moss-covered rock!" as you read the story. Create a puppet show by making stick puppet versions of all the characters in the story. Use a real rock, or draw a rock and attach it to a box to use as a prop for the show.

Leave the moss-covered rock in the room for a few days as a reminder of this great story.

THE ANT AND THE ELEPHANT
by Bill Peet (Houghton Mifflin, 1972).

Story: The biggest and kindest elephant in the jungle rescues an ant, a turtle, a giraffe, a lion, and a rhino. However, the ant is the only one who appreciates the elephant's kindness. When the elephant falls into a deep ravine, his kindness is returned as 95,000 ants carry the elephant to safety.

Materials: a picture of an elephant and a picture of an ant

Directions: Show the elephant and ant to the children and talk about the difference in their sizes. Which creature would be able to help the other if one were in trouble? While reading the story, encourage the children to participate on the "Heave ho!" chanting.

Pin the elephant and ant on the bulletin board as a reminder that in the jungle it is sometimes the survival of the nicest.

ANTS CAN'T DANCE
by Ellen Jackson, il. by Frank Remkiewicz (Macmillan, 1991).

Story: Jonathan's parents don't believe him when he says that he found an ant who can tap dance. The ant will not perform for anyone except Jonathan. The boy also finds a peanut that talks, but, as is the case with the ant, it only talks to Jonathan. However, when Jonathan finds a whistling stone that won't quit whistling, the two become famous.

Materials: stone, whistle, peanuts in shell, marker, ant puppet (see Bug Crafts)

Directions: Draw a face on a peanut shell. After reading the story, bring out the peanut and pretend that it's talking. Do likewise with a stone and whistle. Manipulate the ant puppet to make it tap dance. Let the children use these props when retelling the story, or provide craft materials for children to create their own versions.

Teach the children a few tap dancing steps to "Tea for Two," or any favorite tune. Serve peanuts in the shell. For easy cleanup, lay a tarp on the floor for the children to sit on while shelling and eating peanuts.

"I CAN'T" SAID THE ANT
by Polly Cameron (Coward, 1961).

Story: In this rhyming book (also available as a Big Book) an ant and two spiders help repair the broken spout of a teapot. Everything in the kitchen assists by offering advice.

Materials: teapot, tea cups, tea

Directions: Before reading the story, show the children a teapot and ask them who they think might repair it if it should fall and break. Encourage the children to join in on the reading by naming the illustrations as they appear. This is especially effective with a Big Book on an easel while reading.

After reading the story, hold a tea party, as fancy or as simple as you like.

TWO BAD ANTS

by Chris Van Allsburg (Houghton Mifflin, 1988).

Story: A colony of ants travels into unknown territory to gather crystals for the queen ant. Two bad ants desert the others and stay to eat the delicious crystals. Subsequently, they have several dangerous adventures that encourage them to return to the safety of their home.

Materials: colony of ants (available at most teacher education supply stores or in variety stores)

Directions: Characteristic of Chris Van Allsburg's books, the illustrations reveal the happenings in the story and must be shown as the story is read. It may be best, though, to read through the story completely the first time, for continuity, and then let the children view the intriguing illustrations during the second reading for more complete under-standing. Encourage the children to watch the ants in the ant colony build their home.

THE VERY BUSY SPIDER

by Eric Carle (Scholastic, 1984).

Story: In this story, a little spider is so intent on spinning its web that it ignores all the animals who ask it to stop and play. At the end of the day, it catches a fly in its web, but the spider falls asleep from exhaustion. The web strands in the book are raised, allowing the children to feel the web patterns.

Materials: non-fiction materials about spiders, spider puppet (see Bug Crafts)

Directions: Use a spider puppet to introduce this story. The children will enjoy making animal sounds as each animal appears in the story. Later, make the book available for each child to feel the raised webs. Allow each child to make his or her own busy spider and raised web following the directions in Bug Crafts. Display some non-fiction materials about spiders and their habits.

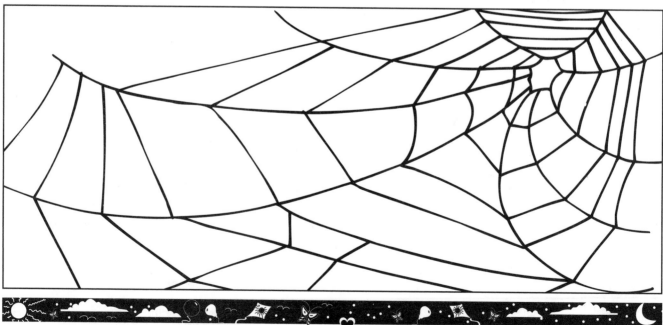

THE VERY HUNGRY CATERPILLAR
by Eric Carle (Scholastic, 1987).

Story: The very hungry caterpillar eats its way right through the pages of this book. It eats an apple on Monday, two pears on Tuesday, and so on, right through the week. Finally, it becomes a very big caterpillar and makes a cocoon. Eventually, it emerges as a beautiful butterfly.

Materials: caterpillar (see Bug Crafts), pieces of fruit to match the fruit in the story

Directions: As you read, encourage the children to join in on the counting of the food the caterpillar devours. Use the caterpillar and fruit to retell the story a second time. Make the props available for the children to tell the story themselves. Encourage them to tell the story to someone. Refer to Bulletin Board Ideas for suggestions on how to make a different very hungry caterpillar and a butterfly.

THE VERY QUIET CRICKET
by Eric Carle (Philomel, 1990).

Story: A newborn cricket meets a big cricket who chirps a welcome by rubbing its wings together. The newborn wants to respond, but there's no sound when it rubs its wings together. The little cricket wants to greet a locust, a praying mantis, a worm, a spittlebug, a cicada, and a bumblebee, but it's not until he matures and meets a female cricket that he is able to chirp. As the last page is turned, a chirping sound is heard from a device concealed in the book.

Materials: cricket puppet (see Bug Crafts)

Directions: The children will enjoy participating in the reading of this story by repeating the refrain "But nothing happened. Not a sound." Hold up the cricket puppet and explain that when the wings rub together, the chirping sound is created. Encourage the children to imitate the chirping as they manipulate the puppet's wings; they may also want to make their own puppets. Remind the children to listen on a warm summer night for crickets chirping outside their bedroom windows.

WHY MOSQUITOES BUZZ IN PEOPLE'S EARS

by Verna Aardema, il. by Diane and Leo Dillon (Scholastic, 1975).

Story: In this West African folk tale, Mosquito tells Iguana a tall tale that starts off a chain reaction of rumors. Mother Owl refuses to hoot to wake the sun and the jungle is left in darkness. Finally, Mosquito learns her lesson, but she adopts another annoying habit, buzzing in people's ears.

Materials: modeling clay, poster paper, crayons and markers

Directions: After reading this story, ask the children to buzz like a mosquito. To make the book come alive, have the children create a large diorama. They can make the jungle animals from clay and use large poster paper to draw a background. Later, hold a game of "Gossip." Ask one child to be Mosquito and another to be Iguana. Have them sit next to each other in a circle of all the children. Mosquito whispers a phrase to Iguana, who passes it on until it reaches the last person, who repeats it aloud.

A WORM'S TALE

by Barbro Lindgren, il. by Cecilia Torudd (Farrar, 1988).

Story: Arthur, a most proper gentleman, doesn't have any friends until he accidentally meets Charles, a worm. Arthur takes Charles to a tailor to get him properly outfitted in blue overalls and a red cap and then their adventures begin.

Materials: white cake mix, whipping cream, strawberries, poster paper, markers, scissors, modeling clay

Directions: Draw Charles on poster paper, then color and cut out. Set him in a modeling clay base. Introduce him to the children as Charles, your very best worm friend. Later, provide the children with materials they can use to make their own worms. Encourage the children to retell the story using their own worm friends as props. For a special treat, serve strawberry-topped cupcakes. Make a white cake mix into cupcakes. Top with whipped cream and fresh, sliced strawberries.

Brinckloe, Julie. **FIREFLIES!** (Macmillan, 1985).

On a warm summer evening, a young boy and his friends run about to gather fireflies in jars. Later, the boy decides to let the fireflies go free.

Brown, Ruth. **IF AT FIRST YOU DO NOT SEE** (Holt, Rinehart, and Winston, 1982).

A hungry caterpillar sets out to find something good to eat. On its scary journey, it discovers that things aren't what they appear to be. The reader must turn the book around to read all four sides of the pages.

Carle, Eric. **THE GROUCHY LADYBUG** (Harper & Row, 1986).

An ill-tempered ladybug challenges all sorts of creatures to fight, but then it finds reasons not to fight. Finally, a whale slaps the ladybug back to the start of its journey, where it meets a friendly ladybug.

Carter, David A. **HOW MANY BUGS IN A BOX?** (Simon & Schuster, 1988).

The reader counts the many wonderfully silly bugs in the various boxes as the lids are opened. There are three bugs in the polka-dot box; five yellow, mellow fish-bugs and a monster in the blue box; and nine long-necked purple bugs in the thin box. Wow!

Conklin, Gladys, il. by Barbara Latham. **I LIKE CATERPILLARS** (Holiday House, 1958).

A little girl goes on a search for caterpillars and explains her reasons for liking each one. She encounters many kinds of caterpillars, including cabbage, viceroy, tent, looper, arctid, and more.

Conklin, Gladys, il. by Artur Marokvia. **WE LIKE BUGS** (Holiday House, 1962).

A young child talks about dragonflies, stinkbugs, tumblebugs, and others as he finds them along the roadside, in vacant lots, and in his backyard.

Dorros, Arthur. **ANT CITIES** (Crowell, 1987).

The ants are busy working. The queen ant lays eggs, the worker ants care for the eggs, and other ants gather food and dig the nest, which is their city.

Gackenbach, Dick. **LITTLE BUG** (Houghton Mifflin, 1981).

Little Bug lives in a dark, dreary hole where he is safe from the dangers of pecking birds and people's sneakers. But then a mysterious voice reminds Little Bug that the pleasures of the world are worth taking a few risks.

Graham, Margaret Bloy. **BE NICE TO SPIDERS** (Harper & Row, 1967).

When Billy moves away, he leaves his pet spider Helen at the zoo. The zoo keeper believes Helen's webs should be torn down until he realizes the webs catch pesky flies. Helen becomes the hero of the zoo.

Hawes, Judy. **FIREFLIES IN THE NIGHT** (Crowell, 1963).

A little girl and her grandparents sit outside on a warm summer night to watch and catch fireflies. They count their flashing signals and gather them in a jar. When it's bedtime, they set the fireflies free.

Johnson, Dolores. **THE BEST BUG TO BE** (Macmillan, 1992).

Kelly is disappointed when she gets the role of a bumblebee instead of the lead

in the school play. She's jealous of her friends who are chosen to play in the ladybug band and to be butterflies that dance on their toes. Then Kelly decides to be the best bumblebee she can be and ends up stealing the show.

Kent, Jack. **THE CATERPILLAR AND THE POLLIWOG** (Prentice-Hall, 1982).

A caterpillar boasts that it will turn into a beautiful butterfly when it grows up. A polliwog watches so intently as the caterpillar changes that it neglects to notice that it has changed also—into a frog.

Lobel, Arnold. **GRASSHOPPER ON THE ROAD** (Harper & Row, 1978).

Grasshopper hops slowly down the road, where it encounters some funny characters—a housefly who is trying to clean the entire world, a worm who lives in an apple, some narrow-minded beetles, and a seafaring mosquito.

Lord, John Vernon and Janet Burroway. **THE GIANT JAM SANDWICH** (Houghton Mifflin, 1972).

On a hot summer day, four million wasps fly into the town of Itching Down. They dive and buzz and drive the villagers crazy. The villagers decide to make a giant strawberry jam sandwich to capture the annoying wasps.

Maxner, Joyce, il. by William Joyce. **NICHOLAS CRICKET** (Harper & Row, 1989).

Nicholas Cricket plays all night long in the Bug-A-Wug Cricket Band. The music is just grand, and all the forest creatures join in on the celebration. The ladybugs strut, the grasshoppers sway, and the snap turtles swing.

McNulty, Faith, il. by Bob Marstall. **THE LADY AND THE SPIDER** (Harper & Row, 1986).

A spider lives comfortably on a lettuce leaf in a lady's garden. One day, the lady picks the lettuce leaf and is about to throw the spider into the trash, but she likes the spider and returns it to another lettuce leaf in her garden.

Mizumura, Kazue. **IF I WERE A CRICKET** (Crowell, 1973).

In this book, the reader journeys through the world of nature to visit a cricket, a snail, a spider, a firefly, and other small creatures.

Oppenheim, Joanne, il. by S. D. Schindler. **EENCY WEENCY SPIDER** (Bantam, 1991).

After the Eency Weency Spider climbs the water spout, it goes off to frighten Miss Muffet, cause Humpty Dumpty to fall, crawl into Little Jackie Horner's cherry pie, and frighten poor Jack-be-nimble, who jumps over the candlestick.

Parker, John, il. by Rita Parkinson. **I LOVE SPIDERS** (Ashton Scholastic, 1988).

In this rhyming book, a variety of intriguing spiders are introduced to the reader. There are shy spiders, bold spiders, fat spiders, oval spiders, and more. I LOVE SPIDERS is also available as a Big Book.

Parker, Nancy Winslow and Joan Richard Wright. **BUGS** (Greenwillow, 1987).

This colorful book includes information, jokes, and descriptions of many common insects. It tells the physical characteristics, habits, and natural environment of each bug.

Pollock, Penny, il. by Lorinda Bryan Cauley. **ANTS DON'T GET SUNDAY OFF** (Putnam, 1978).

Anya is a hard-working ant who longs for a day off and a new adventure. When a heavy rainstorm disturbs her home, she must leave. However, the adventure she embarks upon is more than she expected.

Ryder, Joanne, il. by Lynne Cherry. **THE SNAIL'S SPELL** (Warne, 1982).

A young girl imagines what it's like to be a snail. She pictures herself two inches long, gliding on the cool ground very slowly, eating tiny bits of lettuce by sticking out her tongue, and stretching her feelers to touch everything along the pathway.

Quackenbush, Robert. **HENRY'S AWFUL MISTAKE** (Parents, 1980).

Henry creates a disaster in his kitchen when he tries to get rid of an ant before his friend Clara arrives for dinner.

Stadler, John. **HOORAY FOR SNAIL!** (Crowell, 1984).

Snail hits the baseball so hard that it flies to the moon. Still, poor snail moves very slowly, and must try to reach home base before the ball returns. Luckily, Snail succeeds and wins the game.

Stevenson, James. **NATIONAL WORM DAY** (Greenwillow, 1990).

A worm, a snail, a mole, and a rhinoceros are all friends. They celebrate National Worm Day together, go on walks, and help each other out in times of need.

Van Laan, Nancy, il. by Marisabina Russo. **THE BIG FAT WORM** (Knopf, 1987).

In this rhythmic chain of events, a big fat bird finds a big fat worm he wants to eat, but the worm crawls into the ground. Likewise, a cat finds the bird and a dog finds the cat. All manage to escape each other.

Wagner, Jenny, il. by Ron Brooks. **ARANEA: A STORY ABOUT A SPIDER** (Bradbury, 1975).

The spider Aranea spends her life weaving webs. Sometimes she tears them down to hide in a curling leaf. Sometimes schoolboys break her webs or ladies flick them away from their faces. But the hard-working Aranea always weaves another web.

☀ ☾ Bug Poems & Finger Plays ☽ ☾

AT EARLY MORN

At early morn the spiders spin,
And by and by the flies drop in;
And when they call, the spiders say,
Why don't you stay all day!
—Mother Goose

FIDDLE-DE-DEE

Fiddle-de-dee, fiddle-de-dee,
The fly shall marry the bumblebee.
They went to church, and married was
   she:
The fly has married the bumblebee.
—Mother Goose

LITTLE MISS MUFFET

Little Miss Muffet,
Sat on a tuffet
Eating of curds and whey:
There came a great spider
That sat down beside her,
And frightened Miss Muffet away.
—Mother Goose

More Bug Poems

"I Want You to Meet. . . ," p. 8 and "The Caterpillar," p. 77, in SING A SONG OF POPCORN, selected by Beatrice Schenk de Regniers et al. (Scholastic, 1988).

"Mosquito" and "Lovely Mosquito," p. 21 and "A Bug Sat in a Silver Flower," p. 28, in FOR LAUGHING OUT LOUD, selected by Jack Prelutsky, Priceman (Knopf, 1991).

"Robin Spied a Chubby Worm," p. 28, "Patter, Pitter Caterpillar," p. 34, and "Red Bug, Yellow Bug, Little Blue Snake," p. 48, in BENEATH A BLUE UMBRELLA by Jack Prelutsky (Greenwillow, 1990).

"Fuzzy Wuzzy, Creepy Crawly," "Only My Opinion," and "Ants," p. 62, "Grass-hopper Green," "Dragonfly," and "But I Wonder. . . ," p. 63, and "Under the

Ground," p. 73, in READ-ALOUD RHYMES FOR THE VERY YOUNG, selected by Jack Prelutsky, il. by Marc Brown (Knopf, 1986).

"The Spider and the Fly," p. 37, in ONE THOUSAND POEMS FOR CHILDREN, selected by Elizabeth Hough Sechrist (Macre-Smith, 1946).

CREEPY CRAWLY CRITTER RIDDLES by Joanne E. Bernstein and Paul Cohen, il. by Rosekrans Hoffman (Albert Whitman, 1986).

MY FRIENDLY CATERPILLAR

My friendly caterpillar
(Fingers crawl up arm.)
Made its cocoon one day.
(Close hands together.)
It turned into a butterfly
(Open hands with thumbs hooked
   together.)
And quickly flew away.
(Flap hands.)

EENCY WEENCY SPIDER

An eency weency spider
(Move opposite thumbs and index
   fingers together.)
Climbed up the water spout.
(Climb fingers up.)
Down came the rain and washed the
   spider out.
(Hands sweep downward.)
Out came the sun and dried up all the
   rain
(Arms form circle for sun.)
And the eency weency spider climbed
   up the spout again.
(Repeat climbing action.)
—Mother Goose

BE A BUG

Have the children pretend to be worms and inch around on the floor or be butterflies and flap their wings. Let the children choose which bug to be.

MAKE A WEB

Have four or five children sit in a circle on the floor. Give them a ball of black yarn. One child holds on to the end and then tosses the ball to another child. That child holds the spot and tosses the yarn ball to another, and the game continues with the yarn tossed again and again until a web is made. To end the game, have the children reverse the sequence and wind the yarn back into a ball. As the children are making the web, they may want to sing "The Eency Weency Spider" or retell a spider story.

SPIDER LEGS

(Tune: "Hokey Pokey"; use appropriate actions)

Put your spider legs in,
Put your spider legs out,
Put your spider legs in,
And shake them all about.
Catch a fly and spin a web,
And turn yourself around.
That's what it's all about!
Put your cricket wings in,
Put your cricket wings out,
Put your cricket wings in,
And shake them all about.
You fly like a cricket,
And turn yourself around.
That's what it's all about!
Put your snail head in,
Put your snail head out,
Put your snail head in,

And shake it all about.
You creep into your shell,
And slither all around.
That's what it's all about!
—Stephanie Riggers

CATCH A BUG

Children form a circle by joining hands. Choose two or three children to be the bugs inside the circle (web), and one to be the leader. Have the children in the circle raise their arms to let the bugs go in and out until a special signal is given from the leader to lower their arms quickly to trap the bugs in the web. Continue to play until everyone has been given a chance to be a bug.

LITTLE MISS MUFFET

Encourage the children to dramatize "Little Miss Muffet." Give a plastic bowl and spoon to Miss Muffet to use as props and let a second child pretend to be a spider. Give each child a chance to play both parts.

THE GROUCHY LADYBUG

You will need 14 children to dramatize this story: 2 ladybugs and 12 creatures that the Grouchy Ladybug encounters on its journey. Designate a beginning area. Place the "creatures" in proper sequence. It would add to the fun to have the ladybugs wear costumes (see Bug Crafts). Let the children playing creatures make paper plate masks of the creatures they are pretending to be.

At first, designate one child to be the narrator while the others act, but encourage each child to eventually speak his or her own lines.

Bug Crafts

ANT PUPPET

Materials: ant pattern, pipe cleaners, black or red paper, scissors, string, stapler, markers

Directions: Use the pattern to cut an ant for each child from colored paper. For small children, cut around the entire outline instead of trying to cut out all the little parts. Show the children how to cut six legs from pipe cleaners for their ant and insert into the body as marked. Have them draw on features. Staple two strings onto the back of each ant to make it move. Use this puppet in conjunction with the reading of ANTS CAN'T DANCE.

CRICKET PUPPET

Materials: cricket patterns, brown paper, Popsicle sticks, brads, glue, scissors

Directions: Use the patterns provided to cut out two crickets and one set of wings for each child; for small children it's best to cut around the whole pattern rather than to try to cut out the small parts. Have the children glue the two crickets together with a Popsicle stick between them to make a double-sided puppet. Show the children how to cut out the wings and attach them to the body as indicated on the pattern. The wings may be rubbed together as the children furnish the cricket sound.

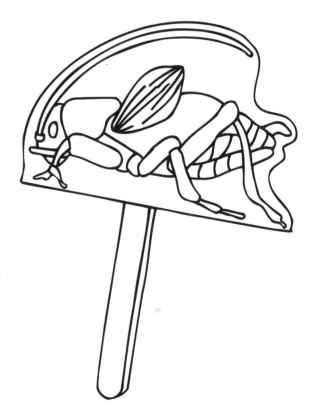

EARTHWORM HOME

Materials: narrow jar with lid (peanut butter or jam jars work well), knife, variety of soils, decayed leaves, worms, water

Directions: Punch a few holes in the lid of the jar. Fill the jar with layers of different-colored soil such as bone meal, sand, earth, peat, and compost. Add some decayed leaves for the pet worm to eat. Keep the worm's house cool and moist but be sure not to over water so the worm doesn't drown. Find a worm by digging in cool, moist soil. Put the worm on top of the soil in its new home and watch it burrow through the layers of soil. Encourage the children to watch and study the worm's habits. After about two weeks, return the worm to its natural home.

CATERPILLAR

This is a great project in which to enlist parent volunteers who like to sew.

Materials: fabric scraps (green and red), felt scraps (yellow, green, and red), yarn or embroidery thread (red and yellow), scissors, fiber fill, thread and needle, hot glue gun

Directions: For each caterpillar, cut six six-inch circles from green fabric. Stitch and gather the edge of each circle, forming a ball. Stuff each ball with fiber fill and stitch closed. Glue a small circle of green felt over the closing stitches. Follow the same instructions to construct one red felt ball for each caterpillar's head. Join the body parts and the head by hand stitching the balls together. Use yellow and green felt to add eyes. Cut two red felt antennae. Put glue on the narrow end of each and use a pencil or something sharp to stick the antennae into the top of the head. On the top of each green body part, stitch and secure several red and yellow strands of yarn or thread to make feelers. Refer to the Read-Aloud section for suggestions on how to use the caterpillar.

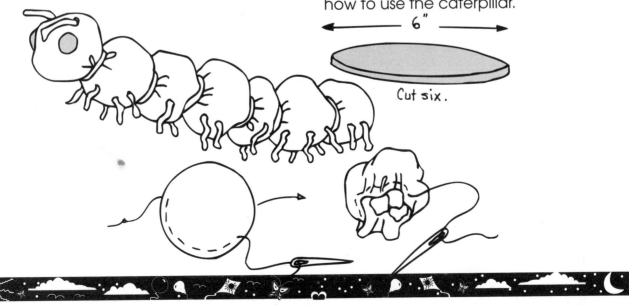

6"

Cut six.

LADYBUGS

Materials: egg cartons, scissors, pipe cleaners, black crayons or markers, red paint, paintbrushes, glue (optional), leaves (optional)

Directions: Cut out egg carton cups. Give each child an individual section to paint red. When the cups are dry, have the children add black spots and insert pipe cleaners for feelers. The children can glue their ladybugs onto real green leaves if desired.

LADYBUG COSTUME

Materials: 2 large pieces of poster paper or cardboard, red and black paint, brushes, scissors, pipe cleaners, black construction paper, stapler, ribbon or yarn

Directions: For each costume, have the children cut two large circles out of the cardboard or poster paper, paint the circles red, and add black dots. Poke holes at the top of each circle and insert a length of ribbon to tie the circles together in a "sandwich" board. Help the children cut a band from black paper 1 1/2" wide by 24" long. Staple the ends together to fit the child's head. Help the children staple pipe cleaners to the band to make the feelers, and they're ready to be ladybugs. A variation would be to use red poster paper and have the children glue on black paper dots.

THE VERY BUSY SPIDER'S WEB

Materials: white construction paper, black tempera paint, squeeze bottles of glue, crayons or markers (optional)

Directions: Mix the paint into partially filled squeeze bottles of glue and let children squeeze the mixture onto paper to create spider webs. The children may want to draw a web first and then follow the lines with the glue. When the webs are dry (two to three days), have the children feel the raised webs. (Children can also squeeze plain white glue onto black paper.)

SPIDER PUPPET

Materials: spider pattern, black paper, Popsicle sticks, glue, scissors

Directions: Use the pattern provided to cut out two black spiders for each puppet. Glue the two spiders together with a Popsicle stick between them to make a double-sided puppet. Use the puppet to dramatize ANANSI AND THE MOSS-COVERED ROCK or any favorite spider story.

POMPON SPIDERS

Materials: black pompons, black pipe cleaners, wiggly eyes, glue, scissors

Directions: Give each child eight equal-size pieces of pipe cleaner to glue onto a pompon for legs. Have them glue on wiggly eyes and let the glue dry. You can substitute painted egg carton cups for the pompons.

SPIDER WEB

Materials: black yarn, white paper, glue, scissors

Directions: Cover a bulletin board with white paper. Glue the yarn onto the paper to form a spider's web. Pin pompon spiders (see above) on the web for a spunky spider display.

Ant Pattern

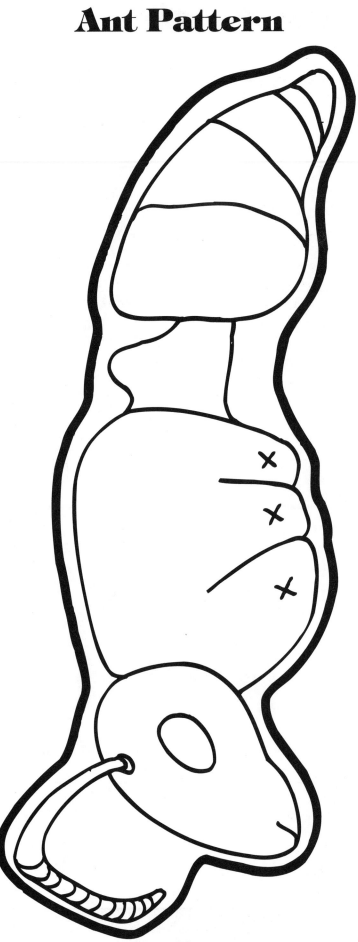

Cricket Pattern

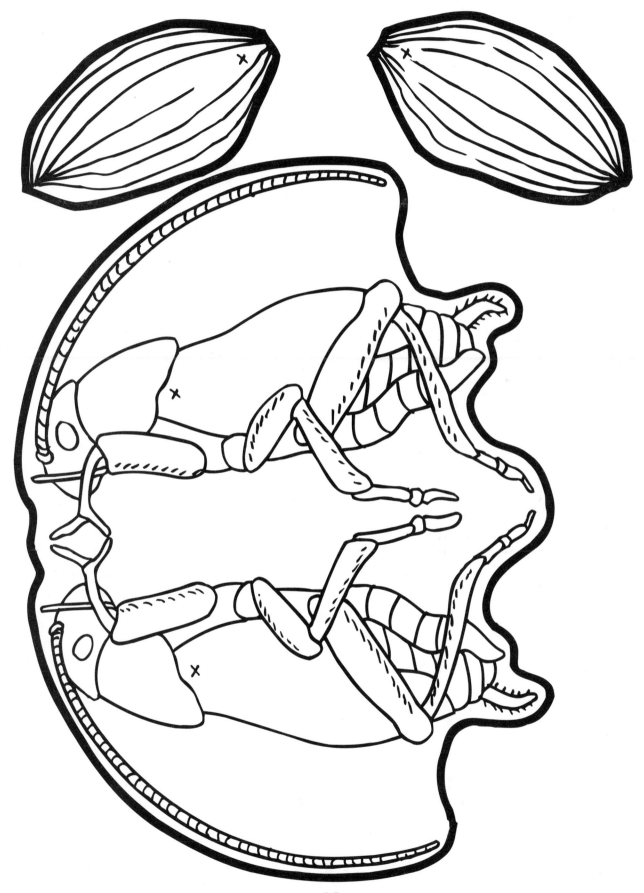

ANTS ON A LOG
(Enjoy this nutritious snack after reading an ant story.)

peanut butter
celery sticks
raisins

Use a table knife to spread peanut butter into the groove of a celery stick (log) and place raisins (ants) on the peanut butter. First show the children how to make the "logs," then let them make their own.

BUGS IN THE MUD
(The children will love it!)

2 cups cold milk
1 package instant chocolate pudding
Gummy worms or any Gummy bugs
7 oz. clear plastic cups

Combine milk and pudding and beat with whisk until thickened. Divide equally into cups and cool in the refrigerator for 1 hour. Just before serving, place the Gummy worms in and on top of the pudding. Makes 4 - 6 servings.

SCRUMPTIOUS SPIDERS

big black gumdrops
black string licorice
edible silver ball cake decorations

Cut the black licorice into eight small pieces and have the children insert them into their gumdrop for the spider legs. Have the children use silver ball decorations for the eyes. Be sure the children eat these spiders quickly before they run away!

BUG COOKIES

Make your favorite sugar cookie recipe. Roll out the dough and cut into circles. A biscuit cutter works well, but a glass will suffice. Frost the cooled cookies with colored, creamy frosting. Then let the children add gumdrops for buggy eyes, round candy for a nose, a butterscotch drop for a mouth, coconut for hair, and string licorice for antennae or legs.

CATERPILLAR CAKE

12 baked cupcakes (adjust for the number you need)
2 cups creamy frosting (adjust for the amount you need)
small gumdrops and a variety of candies
green and yellow food coloring

Add yellow coloring to some of the frosting and frost one of the cupcakes for the head. Add green coloring to the remainder of the icing and frost the other cupcakes. Place the cupcakes together in a wiggly line. Decorate with candies to make eyes, antennae, mouth, nose, feet, and decorations on the caterpillar's back. Let everyone devour part of the caterpiller.

To get the children excited about a clothes-theme unit, hold a hat day! Read books about hats (like THE 500 HATS OF BARTHOLOMEW CUBBINS and CAPS FOR SALE), do the Mexican hat dance, make hats to wear, and have a hat-shaped snack (see Clothes Snacks). Ahead of time, collect hats to keep in a big box to use during dress-up time or dramatic play. Show the children that each time they put on a hat, they can become a new character. You might want to collect a variety of hats that connote different occupations or hobbies: construction worker's hard hat, farmer's hat, baseball cap, football helmet, firefighter's hat, police officer's hat, sailor's cap, detective's hat (like Sherlock Holmes'), railroad engineer's striped cap, white chef's hat, colorful jester's cap, crown for a king or queen, 10-gallon hat, magician's top hat, space helmet, soldier's helmet, party hat, Mexican sombrero, and so on.

Also plan for a shoe day. Read books about shoes, tap dance, and make paper shoes to wear. Provide a shoe collection, which could include tennis shoes, high heels for dress-up, golf shoes, baseball shoes, cowboy boots, slippers, snowshoes, roller skates, thongs, sandals, ballerina slippers, moccasins, tap shoes, galoshes, hiking boots, clogs, or ski boots.

SETTING THE STAGE

Create a paper dolls and clothes center. Don't forget to include some male dolls. In the dress-up center, provide clothes similar to clothes in books. Children will enjoy wearing these while acting out the stories.

In the reading corner, display a sign saying, "Hats Off to Readers," several books about hats, and several hats for the children to wear while reading. Or hang the sign around a stuffed animal who is wearing a hat. Also display a stuffed Corduroy bear near the book A POCKET FOR CORDUROY by Don Freeman. It's a good idea to provide "listening" hats in the reading corner for the children to wear while listening to stories.

BULLETIN BOARD IDEAS

1. Enlarge the illustration "Good Books on the Line," and color and pin it up. Or pin up a piece of rope, cut out shirt patterns from various pieces of fabric, glue book titles onto the shirts, and hang them from the rope with clothespins.

2. Make a "Poem Pocket." Cut two pieces of felt big enough to make a pocket that will hold copies of poems. Decorate the pocket or add a flap and button. Keep poems in the pocket for the children to take and keep in their own pockets and then read with a friend or parent. Occasionally remove a poem from the pocket to share with the children. Nearby, pin up a copy of "Keep a Poem in Your Pocket" by Beatrice Schenk de Regniers.

3. Purchase and pin up a "Cat in the Hat" poster. This Dr. Seuss character is also available in bookstores as a stuffed animal.

4. Copy the poems "Tight Hat" and "Hat" from WHERE THE SIDEWALK ENDS by Shel Silverstein, and "Watermelon Hat" from RIDE A PURPLE PELICAN by Jack Prelutsky. Color, if desired, and pin up after reading each poem to the children.

5. Enlarge, copy, and display an illustration of the delightful Quangle Wangle hat from the book THE QUANGLE WANGLE'S HAT by Edward Lear.

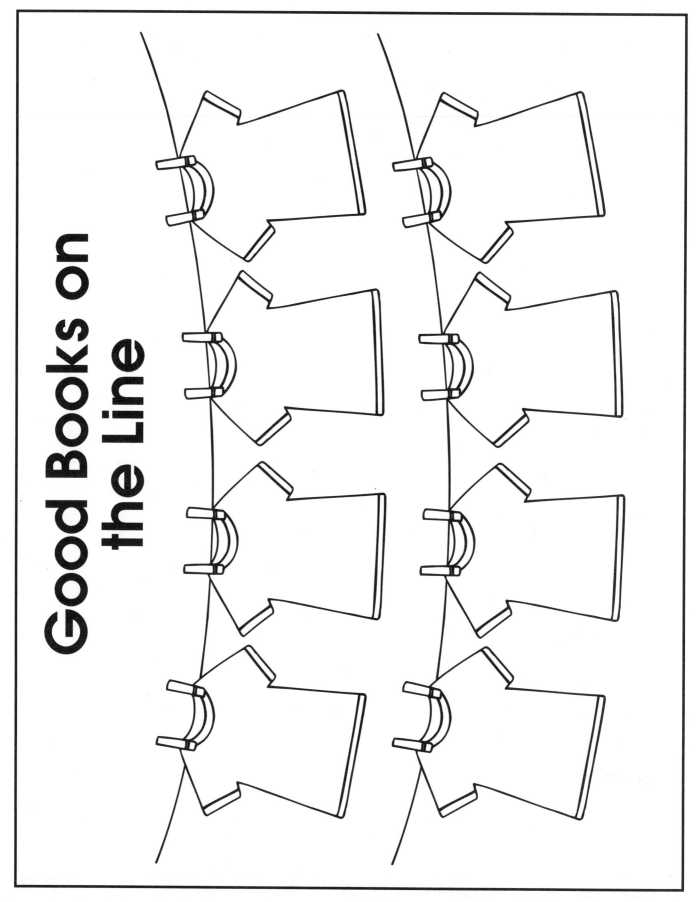

Good Books on the Line

HO FOR A HAT!
by William Jay Smith, il. by Lynn Munsinger (Little, Brown, 1989).

Story: In this delightful rhyme, a young boy and his dog try on a variety of hats—every kind of hat ever invented. There are hats to keep off the sun, hats that fold up, and hats made of silk, wool, straw, and tin.

Materials: a variety of hats as described in the story

Directions: As you read the story, the children will delight in joining in on the "Ho for a hat!" refrain. At the conclusion of the story, throw the collection of hats into the air (as done in the story) and let each child chose a hat to wear for the remainder of the story hour. Each child will want to explain what kind of hat he or she is wearing. Later in the hour, encourage the children to trade hats. Keep the hats in the room for use during dramatic play.

JENNIE'S HAT
by Ezra Jack Keats (Harper & Row, 1966).

Story: Jennie dreams about having a beautiful hat with big flowers. When her aunt sends her a plain hat, Jennie's quite disappointed. She wanders off to the park to feed the birds, and while she's there the birds decorate her hat with flowers, leaves, a nest, and cards.

Materials: straw hat, glue, hat accessories

Directions: While reading this story, use lots of facial expression (sad, envious, and happy). Later, ask the children to make these expressions with you. As a class project, create Jennie's hat. Choose someone to wear the plain hat while the others, one at a time, pretend to be birds decorating it while the story is told again. Take time to glue the objects on. Use light objects like paper flowers and ribbons that will stay on with glue. Refer to Clothes Crafts for additional ideas.

JESSE BEAR, WHAT WILL YOU WEAR?

by Nancy White Carlstrom, il. by Bruce Degen (Macmillan, 1986).

Story: In this rhymed text, Jesse Bear relates what he will wear throughout the day. In the morning, he wears a red shirt and pants that dance. At noon, he has sand on his hand and rice in his hair, and at night, pajamas with feet and sleep in his eyes.

Materials: Jesse Bear's clothes (red shirt, blue shorts, pajamas, and bib), Mother Bear's white apron, Father Bear's tie and vest

Directions: Ask the children to name the color of something they're wearing. Then let the children take turns calling out a word that rhymes ("red" and "bed," "blue" and "shoe," "green" and "lean"). Ask them to listen for rhyming words in the story. Encourage the children to participate in the refrain "Jesse Bear, what will you wear?" Place the clothing items listed above in the dress-up corner for the children to use when retelling the story. They may want to create their own stories, too.

MARTIN'S HATS

by Joan W. Blos (Morrow, 1984).

Story: Martin's hats allow him to become an explorer, an engineer, a chef, a firefighter, and more on his imaginary journey. When it's time for bed, he finds a special hat waiting for him . . . his night cap.

Materials: a variety of hats

Directions: Before beginning the story, explain that to go on the journey told in this book you need special hats. As you read the story, put on the appropriate hat for each adventure. If you don't have every hat necessary, just use the ones you can find. The children can participate by naming the hats as you put them on. Later, make the hats available for the children to wear on their own imaginary journeys.

MARY WORE HER RED DRESS AND HENRY WORE HIS GREEN SNEAKERS

adapted and il. by Merle Peek (Clarion, 1985).

Story: In this popular children's song, Katy Bear's animal friends come to her birthday party wearing different colored clothes. Mary Squirrel wears a red dress; Henry Raccoon wears green sneakers; Amanda Rabbit wears a brown bandanna, and so on. Katy forgets to take off her pink party hat and wears it to bed.

Materials: pink party hats (see Clothes Crafts), cake, dress-up clothes

Directions: Instead of reading this story, sing it. The music is included at the end of the book. Sing the song a second time, and ask the children to join you. Hold a birthday party. Beforehand, ask a volunteer to bake and decorate a cake. Explain to the children that you're going to have a birthday party and designate a place for it. As the children come to the party, have everyone sing a verse about something each child is wearing. Have the children put on the party hats they made earlier, and then bring in the birthday cake as a surprise.

In the dress-up corner, provide the articles of clothing mentioned in the story for use during dramatic play. Spray-paint some old shoes for the green sneakers.

THE MONSTER AND THE TAILOR

retold and il. by Paul Galdone (Clarion, 1982).

Story: The Grand Duke promises to give the tailor a bag of gold if he will stitch a pair of lucky trousers in the graveyard at night. A horrible creature appears, but the tailor overcomes his fear and finishes the trousers in time.

Materials: the Grand Duke's trousers (see below), candle in candlestick, matches

Directions: When reading this story, create lots of excitement during the scene when the monster chases the tailor. Use a "monster-type" voice for the monster dialogue, and don't forget to tremble when the tailor trembles. To add some special effects, darken the room before beginning the story, and light and blow out the candle when the tailor does in the story. Beforehand, create a pair of yellow and orange trousers similar to the Grand Duke's. They could be sewn from fabric or drawn, colored, and cut from poster paper. In either case, at the end of the story, bring out the lucky trousers to show the children. Post the trousers somewhere in the room as a reminder of the wonderful story.

THE RAG COAT
by Lauren Mills (Little, Brown, 1991).

Story: The Quilting Mothers gather at Minna's house to make her a coat from scraps of fabric. Minna wears her rag coat proudly, but the children laugh at her funny coat until she tells the stories related to each scrap of fabric.

Materials: rag coat pattern (see Clothes Crafts), fabric, markers

Directions: Ask each child to bring a scrap of fabric to show and tell. Whose fabric is it, what was made from it, and where did the fabric come from? Encourage the children to tell each other the history of their fabric scrap. After reading THE RAG COAT, refer to Clothes Crafts for ideas for making a fabric rag coat with the children. Or give each child a coat pattern and markers and let them design their own winter wear.

ROSEBUD AND RED FLANNEL
by Ethel Pochocki, il. by Mary Beth Owens (Holt, 1989).

Story: Red Flannel, a pair of red, woolen long johns, and Rosebud, a delicate, lacy nightgown, hang on the clothesline side by side on wash days. Red Flannel loves Rosebud, but Rosebud feels it is beneath her dignity to converse with a pair of long johns. However, when they are both blown away in a snowstorm, they discover true love.

Materials: materials for paper long johns and nightgowns (see Clothes Crafts), real red long johns, a delicate nightgown, rope or clothesline

Directions: Hang a pair of red long johns and a delicate nightgown on a clothesline strung across a corner of the room. Leave them up for a few days to arouse the children's curiosity. After reading the story, the children will want to make their own paper long johns and nightgowns. The children can use these as props when retelling the story.

Andersen, Hans Christian, retold and il. by Nadine Bernard Westcott. **THE EMPEROR'S NEW CLOTHES** (Little, Brown, 1984).

Two swindlers come to the emperor's castle and pretend to weave fancy clothes that only wise people can see. The emperor loves his new invisible clothes, and wears them during a royal procession. During the parade, a small child calls out that the emperor has no clothes on. At the end of the book, there is a cut-out emperor doll and clothes for him to wear.

Barrett, Judi, il. by Ron Barrett. **ANIMALS SHOULD DEFINITELY NOT WEAR CLOTHING** (Atheneum, 1979).

Lots of trouble happens when animals wear clothes. The porcupine's quills tear the clothes; the snake can't keep up his pants; the sheep gets too hot; the hen can't lay her egg; and so on.

Brett, Jan. **TROUBLE WITH TROLL** (Putnam, 1992).

On a trip up Mount Baldy, Treva and her dog Tuffi meet five white-haired trolls who want Tuffi for their own pet. However, quick-thinking Treva convinces the trolls that her mittens, hat, and sweater are more important than Tuffi, and they take these items of clothing instead.

Calmenson, Stephanie, il. by Denise Brunkus. **THE PRINCIPAL'S NEW CLOTHES** (Scholastic, 1989).

Mr. Bundy, the school principal, loves clothes and is a very sharp dresser. Two tricksters visit the school and offer to make Mr. Bundy a suit from a special cloth which is visible only to the wise. The principal wears his invisible clothes to the assembly, and a kindergarten child calls out that the principal is in his underwear.

Cazet, Denys. **BIG SHOE, LITTLE SHOE** (Bradbury, 1984).

Grandpa and Louie rabbit are happy playing checkers, but when it's time for the laundry to be delivered, Louie wants to go along. Louie trades shoes with Grandpa and convinces him that when he's wearing the big shoes he can help Grandpa in the delivery truck.

de Paola, Tomie. **CHARLIE NEEDS A CLOAK** (Prentice-Hall, 1973).

Charlie, a shepherd, and his favorite sheep enact an hilarious comedy of errors as Charlie sheers his sheep, cards and spins the wool, weaves and dyes his cloth, and cuts out and sews a beautiful red cloak for himself.

de Paola, Tomie. **MARIANNA MAY AND NURSEY** (Holiday House, 1983).

Nursey doesn't allow Marianna May to get her pretty white clothes dirty, so her friends dye all her dresses different colors for different activities.

Ernst, Lisa Campbell. **NATTIE PARSON'S GOOD-LUCK LAMB** (Viking Kestrel, 1988).

Nattie's grandfather decides to sell some lambs. Nattie doesn't like that idea, so she shears her pet lamb Clover, and uses Clover's wool to spin, weave, and sell a beautiful shawl.

Fox, Mem, il. by Patricia Mullins. **SHOES FROM GRANDPA** (Orchard, 1989).

In this cumulative rhyme, young Jessie's family members want to give her socks, a skirt, blouse, sweater, coat, scarf, hat, and mittens to go with the shoes Grandpa has given her. But what Jessie really wants is some new jeans.

Freeman, Don. **DANDELION** (Puffin, 1980).

Dandelion, a vain but lovable lion, overdresses for a come-as-you-are tea party. The hostess turns him away at the door when she doesn't recognize him. From then on Dandelion decides to be himself.

Freeman, Don. **A POCKET FOR CORDUROY** (Viking, 1978).

When Corduroy is visiting the laundro-mat, he hears Liza and her mother talking about pockets. Corduroy wants his own pocket, and while looking for one he's locked in the laundromat overnight. When Liza finds him, she makes a purple pocket for him and gives him a name card to put in it.

Garelick, May, il. by William Pene du Bois. **JUST MY SIZE** (Harper & Row, 1990).

A little girl loves her beautiful blue coat with two big pockets. As she grows, her coat is turned into a jacket, then a vest and cap, a knapsack, and finally a beautiful coat for her doll.

Gelman, Rita Golden, il. by Eric Gurney. **HELLO, CAT YOU NEED A HAT** (Scholastic, 1979).

Told in rhyme, a little mouse attempts to convince a cat to wear a hat. The mouse shows the cat a large variety of hats—rain hats, sun hats, bathing hats, and so on, but each time the cat says no. Finally, the mouse brings out shoes for the cat to wear, and the cat runs away.

Geringer, Laura, il. by Arnold Lobel. **A THREE HAT DAY** (Harper & Row, 1985).

The lonely R. R. Pottle the Third is a collector of hats. He loves his bathing cap, firefighter's hat, and sailor hat. One day he goes to the hat store where he tries on three hats on top of each other and finds a friend who loves hats as much as he does.

Hest, Amy, il. by Amy Schwartz. **THE PURPLE COAT** (Four Winds Press, 1986). A little girl has always had to settle for a plain navy blue coat every fall. But this year she's determined to have something new, a purple coat.

Hindley, Judy, il. by Peter Utton. **UNCLE HAROLD AND THE GREEN HAT** (Farrar, 1991).

Malcolm puts on a green leprechaun hat he finds in his uncle's dental office. It's a magic hat that takes him to whatever place or situation he has in mind. He experiences an avalanche of sweets, then snow, and finally rockets back home in a rocket ship.

Hissey, Jane. **LITTLE BEAR'S TROUSERS** (Philomel, 1987).

Little Bear searches for his lost trousers and then discovers that each of his toys has found a different use for them. The camel wears his pants on his humps, the sailor uses them for a sail on his boat, and the bear fills his pants with frosting to decorate his birthday cake.

Iwamura, Kazuo. **TAN TAN'S HAT** (Bradbury, 1983).

Tan Tan, the little monkey, can do nearly everything with his hat. He can toss it, spin it, and make it do tricks.

Iwamura, Kazuo. **TAN TAN'S SUSPENDERS** (Bradbury, 1983).

Tan Tan's suspenders do much more than hold up his pants. They give him rides, work as a swing, serve as a parachute, and offer more fun than most suspenders can.

Kuskin, Karla. **A BOY HAD A MOTHER WHO BOUGHT HIM A HAT** (Houghton Mifflin, 1976).

A boy's mother buys him a hat, a mouse, shoes, skis, a mask, a cello. and an elephant. He doesn't want any of these things. When he loses his hat in the wind, his mother buys him another, only this one has three points.

Kuskin, Karla, il. by Marc Simont. **THE PHILHARMONIC GETS DRESSED** (Harper & Row, 1982).

Ninety-two men and thirteen women get dressed to go to work—to play in the Philharmonic Orchestra. They bathe, put on their underwear, black socks, white shirts, ties, and so on. When they're ready, they take their instruments to town to play in the evening's performance.

Lear, Edward, il. by Helen Oxenbury. **THE QUANGLE WANGLE'S HAT** (Puffin, 1987).

In this imaginative rhyme, Quangle Wangle lives in the crumpetty tree. His face can't be seen because the beaver hat he wears is much too big—it's a hundred and two feet wide. An assortment of animals (such as the Pobble, who has no toes) comes to live in the beaver hat in the crumpetty tree.

London, Jonathan, il. by Frank Remkiewicz. **FROGGY GETS DRESSED** (Viking, 1992).

Froggy decides to stay up for the winter so he can play in the snow. Each time he goes outside, he forgets an item of clothing. He gets tired from dressing and undressing and decides to sleep for the winter after all.

Meyers, Bernice. **THE FLYING SHOES** (Lothrop, Lee & Shepard, 1992).

Donna and her mother create a pair of flying shoes to give to the queen as a wedding gift. A thief manages to steal the special shoes, but Donna is able to get them back.

Miller, Margaret. **WHOSE SHOE?** (Greenwillow, 1991).

The reader guesses the owner of each pair of shoes pictured—hockey player, clown, baby, horse, etc. A photograph of the wearer appears on the following page. WHOSE HAT? is a similar book by the same author.

Neitzel, Shirley, il. by Nancy Winslow. **THE DRESS I'LL WEAR TO THE PRESS** (Greenwillow, 1992).

In this cumulative rhyme, a little girl dons a wild print dress, shiny black pumps, and creative accessories to get ready for a party. However, when her mother sees the outfit, she reclaims everything and dresses her more appropriately.

Nodset, Joan L., il. by Fritz Siebel. **WHO TOOK THE FARMER'S HAT?** (Scholastic, 1963).

The farmer's big brown hat blows away in the wind. He hunts everywhere for it and asks a squirrel, a fly, and others for help in his search. Finally, he finds his hat in a tree where a bird is using it for a nest. The farmer decides to leave it there and buys himself another brown hat.

Otey, Mimi. **DADDY HAS A PAIR OF STRIPED SHORTS** (Farrar, 1990).

A little girl's dad likes to wear mismatched clothes. He wears striped shorts with his flowered Hawaiian shirt.

Sometimes it's embarrassing when he appears in public wearing these odd clothes, but no matter what he wears, everyone likes him.

Primavera, Elise. **A MAN AND HIS HAT** (Philomel, 1991).

An old man cannot find his shabby hat. He and his wife search through the house, only to discover it in a most unexpected place.

Rogers, Jean, il. by Rie Munoz. **RUNAWAY MITTENS** (Greenwillow, 1988).

Pica has some fine red mittens his grandmother knit for him. However, they're always showing up in strange places, and Pica can never find them when he needs them. One day Pica discovers his mittens keeping the new-born puppies warm in their box, so he leaves his mittens there.

Seuss, Dr. **THE CAT IN THE HAT** (Random House, 1957).

On a cold, wet day when the children can't go outside to play, the Cat in the Hat comes into the house and entertains them. A terrible mess is created, but, luckily, all is set right before their mother gets home.

Seuss, Dr. **THE 500 HATS OF BARTHOLO-MEW CUBBINS** (Vanguard, 1938).

Bartholomew's hat is old and battered, but it does have a fine feather. Much to Bartholomew's surprise, every time he takes off his hat there is another on his head. This goes on and on for some time. Finally, the king agrees to purchase the 500th hat for 500 gold pieces, and after that no more hats appear.

Slobodkina, Esphyr. **CAPS FOR SALE** (Scholastic, 1968).

A peddler stacks his caps on top of his head as he walks around calling, "Caps for sale." When he takes a rest under a tree, some monkeys steal his caps. He becomes angry with the monkeys until they give the hats back.

Van Laan, Nancy, il. by Holly Meade. **THIS IS THE HAT: A STORY IN RHYME** (Knopf, 1992).

As a man with a wooden cane walks in the rain, the wind carries his hat away. A spider, a mouse, and a crow inhabit the hat, but eventually the man gets his hat back.

Wallace, Barbara Brooks, il. by John Sanford. **ARGYLE** (Abingdon, 1987).

A Scottish sheep named Argyle turns many different colors after he eats colored flowers. His owner uses Argyle's wool to make plaid socks.

Watson, Pauline, il. by Tomie de Paola. **THE WALKING COAT** (Walker, 1980).

Young Scott wears his cousin's cast-off coat to keep warm. However, the coat is so big that it covers Scott from head to toe. When he wears the coat, it looks as if it's walking by itself.

Mother Goose Rhymes

LITTLE BETTY BLUE

Little Betty Blue lost her holiday shoe;
What can little Betty do?
Give her another to match the other,
And then she may walk out in two.

RED STOCKINGS

Red stockings, blue stockings,
Shoes tied up with silver;
A red rosette upon my breast
And a gold ring on my finger.

LITTLE MISS LILY

Little Miss Lily,
You're dreadfully silly
To wear such a very long skirt.
If you take my advice,
You would hold it up nice
And not let it trail in the dirt.

DAFFY-DOWN-DILLY

Daffy-down-dilly
Has come up to town,
In a yellow petticoat
And a green gown.

THE CAT'S HAT

A fine grey cat
Was very fat,
And when she sat
Upon her hat,
She smashed it flat
And that was that!

OLD MAN OF PERU

There was an old man of Peru
Who dreamed he was eating his shoe.
He woke in the night
In a terrible fright,
And found it was perfectly true.
—Anonymous

More Clothes Poems

"Molly Day," p. 22, "Timmy Tatt," p. 32, and "Watermelon Hat," p. 32, in RIDE A PURPLE PELICAN by Jack Prelutsky, il. by Garth Williams (Greenwillow, 1986).

"Polar Bear," p. 10, in READ-ALOUD RHYMES FOR THE VERY YOUNG, selected by Jack Prelutsky, il. by Marc Brown (Knopf, 1986).

"Hat Plunger," p. 74, and "Tight Hat," p. 83, in WHERE THE SIDEWALK ENDS by Shel Silverstein (Harper & Row, 1974).

☀ Clothes Action Verses and Songs ☽

I PUT MY HAT ON MY HEAD
(Use this verse to develop independence in dressing. Suit actions to words.)

I put my hat on my head,
And tie the strap in a bow.
Next I slip into my coat,
One arm, then the other just so.
My boots to keep my feet dry,
Pull and pull, I'm ready to go.

COBBLER, COBBLER

Cobbler, cobbler, mend my shoe.
Yes, good mother, that I'll do.
(Pound fists together.)
Stitch it up and stitch it down,
(Make imaginary stitches.)
And then I'll give you half a crown.
(Extend hand.)
Cobbler, cobbler, mend my shoe,
(Pound fists together.)
Get it done by half-past two.
(Extend two fingers.)
Half-past two, it can't be done.
Get it done by half-past one.
(Extend one finger.)
—Mother Goose

ONE, TWO, BUCKLE MY SHOE
(Count on fingers and suit actions to words.)

One, two, buckle my shoe,
Three, four, shut the door,
Five, six, pick up sticks,
Seven, eight, lay them straight,
Nine, ten, do it again.
—Unknown

THE THREE LITTLE KITTENS
(Create own tune.)

Three little kittens lost their mittens,
And they began to cry,
"Oh, Mother dear,
We very much fear
That we have lost our mittens."
"Lost your mittens!
You naughty kittens!
Then you shall have no pie."
The three little kittens found their mittens,
And they began to cry,
"Oh, Mother dear
See here, see here!
See, we have found our mittens!"
"Put on your mittens,
You silly kittens,
And you may have some pie."
"Purr-r, purr-r, purr-r,
Oh, let us have some pie!
Purr-r, purr-r, purr-r."
—Unknown

More Clothes Action Verses and Songs

"Little Old Lady," p. 80, "Mr. Haber Dasher," p. 76, "Mr. Tickle Lickle," p. 74, and "Somebody Sat on Barnaby's Hat," p. 112, in MOVE OVER, MOTHER GOOSE by Ruth Dowell, il. by Concetta C. Scott (Gryphon House, 1987).

"I Am a Cobbler," p. 44, "Mitten Weather," p. 60, "Shiny Shoes," p. 82, and "Tying My Shoe," p. 99, in RING A RING O'ROSES: FINGER PLAYS FOR PRE-SCHOOL CHILDREN (Flint Public Library, 1988).

"The Tailor and the Mouse," p. 70, "Shoemaker, Shoemaker," p. 69, "Pop Goes the Weasel," p. 64, "Jennie Jenkins," p. 42, in EYE WINKER, TOM TINKER, CHIN CHOPPER by Tom Glazer (Doubleday, 1973).

Clothes Games and Dramatic Play

MEXICAN HAT DANCE

Invite a dancer to teach some simple steps to do around a sombrero placed on the floor. Use recorded music that grows progressively faster. If a dancer isn't available, the children will enjoy doing their own dance steps around the hat. Provide several sombreros or have the children take turns.

WHO TOOK THE FARMER'S HAT?

To dramatize this story, you'll need two brown hats and eight characters: farmer, squirrel, mouse, fly, goat, duck, bird, and shopkeeper. At first, read the story while the children do the acting. Later, let them tell it by themselves. Give everyone an opportunity to participate by dramatizing the story several times or doubling up on the characters. For instance, have several goats, ducks, and so on until all children have had a part.

HATS ON THE FENCE

Materials: some old hats, 3 or more beanbags, board (a 2 x 4 about 5' long)

Directions: Place the board between two tables and place the hats on the board. Mark a line on the floor for the children to stand on while trying to knock off the hats with the beanbags. Play this game just for fun—to see how many hats can be knocked off—so that everyone is a winner.

DRESS UP FOR FUN

Divide players into groups of three or four. Put the groups in different rooms or corners so they won't see each other. Give each group a roll of toilet tissue. The players work together to dress one player up using the toilet tissue. When they're finished, have the dressed-up children come to the center of the room so everyone can see the costumes. Vote for the cutest costume, the most original, the most unique, and so on.

DRESS-UP RELAY

Divide the children into two or more groups. Line each group up behind a chair. Place another chair about 15 feet away. Give each group an oversized T-shirt. The first player in each group puts on the shirt, runs to the other chair, runs back to the next player in line, and gives the shirt to that player to wear. Play continues until everyone has partic-ipated. Play for fun. Don't name a winning team.

RED FLANNEL AND ROSEBUD

Materials: long johns and nightgown patterns, construction paper, buttons, lace, ribbons, scissors, crayons or markers, glue, rope or clothesline

Directions: Let each child color and cut out a pattern or draw his or her own. The clothes can be decorated with buttons, lace, and ribbon. Have the children draw rosebuds on the nightgowns. Hang the paper clothes from a clothesline, or put them on a stick and use them as props to tell the story.

RECYCLED HAT

This is a great project for teaching children to recycle.

Materials: recyclable materials such as paper cups, ribbon, yarn, pipe cleaners, buttons, paper flowers; glue; tape; stapler

Directions: Provide an assortment of recyclable materials to make hats. If the children need encouragement, tell them to start with a paper cup and glue or tape on accessories. Yarn or ribbon can be stapled to the cup and tied under the children's chin.

PINK PARTY HAT

Make this hat after reading MARY WORE HER RED DRESS AND HENRY WORE HIS GREEN SNEAKERS.

Materials: hat pattern, pink construction paper, scissors, stapler, shredded paper, yarn, glue

Directions: Cut a hat pattern from pink paper for each child. Show the children how to fold them into cone shapes and staple together. Let the children staple or glue the shredded paper to the top. The children may cut out designs to glue onto the hat for decorations. Staple two strands of yarn to each hat to tie together for a chin strap.

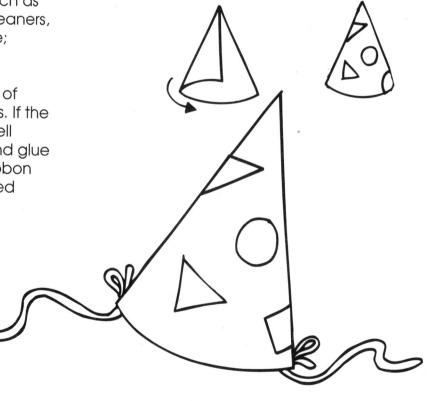

MONSTER FINGERPRINTS

Read THE MONSTER AND THE TAILOR before doing this craft.

Materials: finger paint, large sheet of paper.

Directions: Hang the paper up on the wall at an appropriate height for the children to reach. One at a time, let each child pretend to be the monster in the story, dip his or her hands into the paint, and make monster prints on the paper.

RAG COAT

Materials: coat pattern, fabric scraps, scissors, glue, buttons

Directions: Divide the children into groups of three or four. Enlarge enough coat patterns for each group to have one. Let the children glue the fabric scraps onto the patterns and trim the edges where needed. They can glue on buttons and a collar cut from fabric. This project teaches cooperation.

JENNIE'S HAT

Materials: hat and accessories patterns, crayons or colored markers, scissors, glue, ribbon

Directions: Make enough copies of the hat and accessories for each child. Let the children glue on a strip of ribbon to hang down below the hat. Then they can color the accessories to glue onto the hat.

Nightgown Pattern

Long John Pattern

Hat Pattern

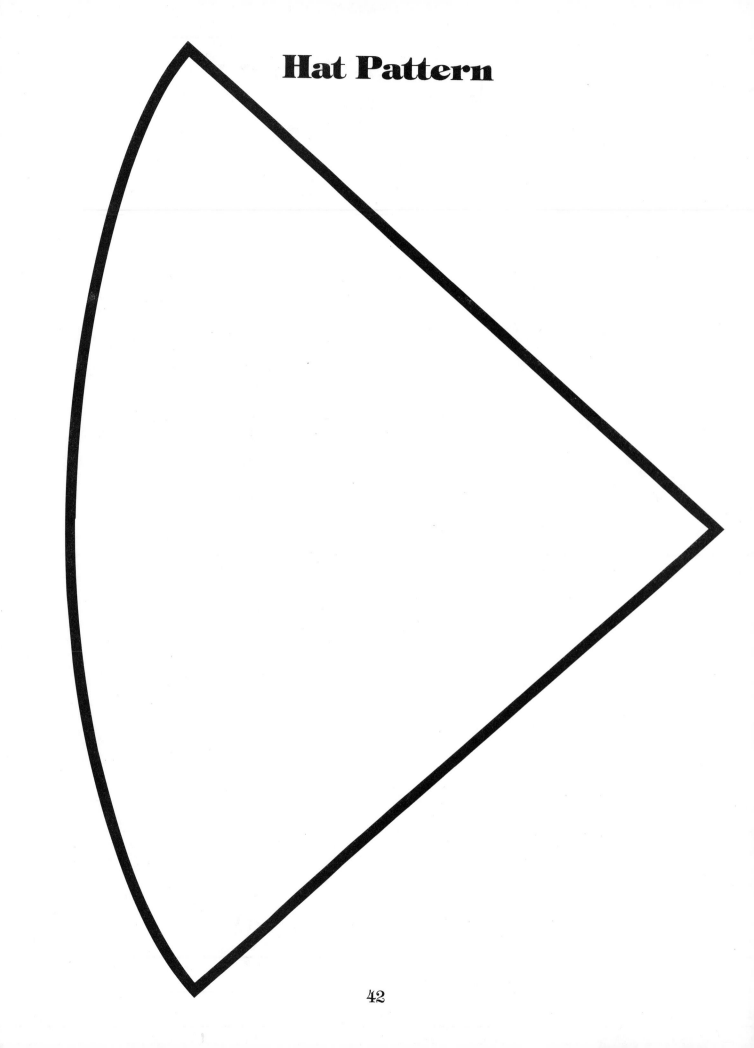

42

Hat Pattern

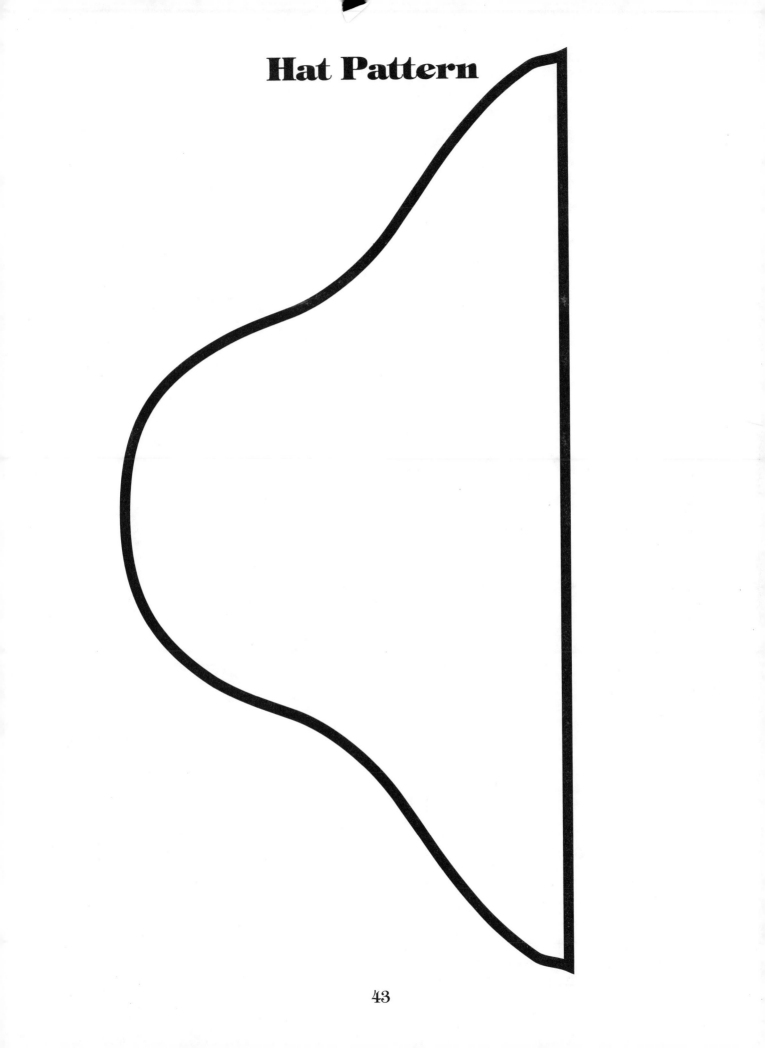

Hat Accessories Patterns

Coat Pattern

SHIRT SANDWICHES

Make the appropriate number of the children's favorite sandwich. Cut a T-shirt pattern that fits the sandwich, place it on each sandwich, and cut them out. Place olive slices down the middle of each for buttons.

ICE CREAM HATS

For each child, place a flat chocolate cookie on a small plate. Top with a scoop of chocolate ice cream to make a hat. A length of string licorice could be wrapped around the ice cream to make a hat band.

HAT CAKE

Make your favorite cake mix or recipe and bake in two 8" round cake pans. Remove the cakes from the pans to cool. Cut a 10"-diameter circle from heavy cardboard. Place the cakes on the cardboard, sealing the layers with frosting. Frost the entire cake and the cardboard to resemble a hat. Put a ribbon around the cake and decorate with candies if desired.

You are never alone with a book. Books can be great friends that travel with you anywhere, make you laugh, give you new ideas, and offer hours of wonderful entertainment. This chapter is filled with ideas to help encourage children to make friends with books, as well as cultivate friendships with other people and understand the importance of friends. Starting the school year with this chapter will set a friendly tone for the entire year.

SETTING THE STAGE

Label a box "Friends" and fill it with stuffed animals and dolls. Next to the box, place two stuffed animals close together holding a sign that says "Happy Friends Day." The children may choose a toy from the box to hold during story hour, or they might like to share a picture book with a new friend.

Encourage the children to become friends with books by offering a reading award certificate to those who read (or have read to them) a designated number of books.

Make various signs to put up around the room or in the reading corner. A few suggestions: "Hug a Friend," "Make Friends with Books," "Best Friends Share Books," "Spend Story Time with Some Good Friends," "The Librarian Is One of My Best Friends," and "A Book Is Your Friend Forever." Designate a "Friend Week" and encourage the children to do things with a friend, such as read a book together or share a snack. Encourage friends to go to the reading corner together.

BULLETIN BOARD IDEAS

1. Enlarge the "Friendship Tree" pattern provided and attach to a bulletin board. The children can bring interesting photos of themselves to attach to the tree. You can also take instant photos of each child, or ask the children to draw pictures of themselves.

2. Pin up a George and Martha poster (available at book stores and through some supply catalogs). Or enlarge, cut out, and color various illustrations of George and Martha from the series by James Marshall. Arrange the pictures with the heading "George and Martha Are Best Friends."

3. Purchase a Winnie-the-Pooh poster that says, "When You Read with a Friend the Adventures Never End." Write to the following address for a catalog of posters: ALA Graphics, American Library Association, 50 East Huron Street, Chicago, IL 60611.

4. Enlarge the illustration "Have You Hugged a Book Today?", included in this chapter. Color, mat, and display.

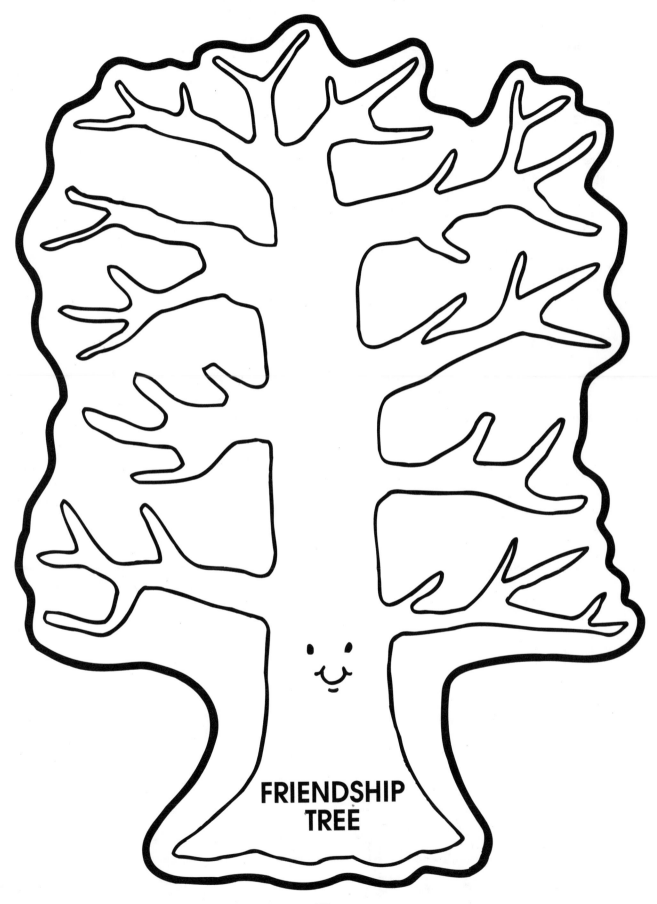

FRIENDSHIP
TREE

ANNA BANANA AND ME
by Lenore Blegvad, il. by Erik Blegvad (Atheneum, 1985).

Story: Fearless Anna Banana isn't afraid of swinging high, of dark hallways, of crawling under bushes, or of an imaginary horrible goblin. But her friend is afraid of all these things until a magic white feather gives him the confidence he needs.

Materials: white feathers

Directions: Ahead of time, hide white feathers in various places around the classroom, or outside, if possible. After reading the story, ask the children to go on a white feather hunt (like an Easter Egg hunt). Make sure that every child has a feather to keep. Discuss nicknames like "Anna Banana." Ask if any of the children has a nickname. Then have fun creating nicknames. Examples: Shelley Jelly, Mandy Candy, Sherie Cherry, Dark Mark, Hot Scott. The children may know the nicknames of some famous people, especially sports stars or musicians: Magic Johnson, Flo Jo, Elvis "The King" Presley.

ANNA'S SECRET FRIEND
by Yoriko Tsutsui, il. by Akiko Hayashi (Viking Kestrel, 1986).

Story: Anna's family moves to a new house near the mountains. She misses her friends, but every day a mysterious person leaves her gifts: flowers, a letter, a paper doll. After a few days, Anna discovers that a little girl has been leaving the gifts because she wants to be Anna's friend.

Materials: violets and dandelions (real or paper), letter similar to the one in the story, paper doll

Directions: Before reading the story, ask the children how they would show someone that they wanted to be friends. When reading the story, make the "tip, tap" sounds when they occur. Sing the phrase "Violets, dandelions, a letter. . ." and ask the children to join in. Hold up the props at the appropriate times. As a follow-up activity, let the children make their own tissue paper violets and dandelions, letters, and paper dolls. They can use these when retelling the story to someone else, a new friend, perhaps.

FOX AND HEGGIE
by Sandra E. Guzzo, il. by Kathy Parkinson (Whitman, 1983).

Story: While Heggie and Fox are shopping, Fox finds a Greek fisherman's cap he wants, but he doesn't have enough money to buy it. Fox's generosity prevents him from saving enough money to buy the cap. To Fox's surprise, his friends pool their money and purchase the cap for him.

Materials: Greek fisherman's cap (see Friend Crafts), a variety of other hats

Directions: It's best to paraphrase this story a little since it may be too long for young listeners. After telling the story, set up a hat shop with a variety of hats, and let the children take turns pretending to purchase hats and act as the hat clerk. Children may want to make caps of their own. This book provides a great lead-in for a lesson on money, counting, and making change.

HOW JOE BEAR AND SAM THE MOUSE GOT TOGETHER
by Beatrice Schenk de Regniers, il. by Bernice Myers (Lothrop, Lee & Shepard, 1965).

Joe and Sam want to be friends. However, they find it difficult because Joe is very big and Sam is quite small, and they have very different ideas about what they like to do. They end up working out their differences over a bowl of ice cream (which they both enjoy).

Materials: two or three different flavors of ice cream, bowls, spoons, and napkins for the entire class

Directions: As the story is read, the children will want to join in on the "Boo hoo's." And, of course, by the end of the tale, everyone will be ready to enjoy some ice cream with a friend (just like Joe and Sam).

I HAVE A FRIEND
by Keiko Narahashi (Atheneum, 1987).

Story: A small boy tells about his very special friend, his shadow. Sometimes his friend is short and fat, and sometimes he's tall enough to touch the trees. His friend goes everywhere with him during the day, but leaves when darkness comes. Happily, his shadow returns with the morning sun.

Materials: sunshine

Directions: Read this book on a sunny day. Take the children outside to find their shadow. The children will want to experiment to see what their shadow can do. Shadows can dance, turn cartwheels, run, take giant steps, and so on.

MAY I BRING A FRIEND?
by Beatrice Schenk de Regniers, il. by Beni Montresor (Atheneum, 1964).

Story: A king and queen invite a small boy to come to their castle on Sunday for tea. The king and queen let the boy bring a friend, and the friend turns out to be a giraffe. On each of the other days of the week, the boy brings a different animal. Finally, on Saturday, the king and queen decide to go to the zoo to have tea with all the animals.

Materials: supplies for a pretend or real tea party, stuffed animals, boy and girl dolls

Directions: As you read the story, have the children join in on the repetitive phrases. Hold a tea party in the play center using the stuffed animals and the boy and girl dolls as the king and queen. Or hold a real tea party with peppermint tea and little cookies. Refer to Friend Songs and Friend Dramatic Play for additional ideas concerning this story.

MY FRIEND THE MOON
by Andre Dahan (Viking, 1987).

Story: A little man rows over the glassy lake to visit the moon as it hangs low in the sky. When the moon falls into the lake, the man dries it off and takes it home to be his friend.

Materials: scissors; construction paper; chalk, crayons, or watercolors; string

Directions: Ask the children to join you in singing "Twinkle, Twinkle Little Star" when it's mentioned in the story. Make a large moon from paper. Shade with chalk, crayons, or watercolors. Hang from the ceiling with a string. Have the children make their own moon to take home.

TACKY THE PENGUIN
by Helen Lester, il. by Lynn Munsinger (Houghton Mifflin, 1988).

Story: Tacky is an odd bird and does not fit in with his graceful companions. However, when the hunters come to capture the penguins, Tacky's odd behavior comes in handy. All of the penguins agree that it's nice to have a friend like Tacky. (Also available on cassette tape.)

Materials: penguin puppet dressed like Tacky (see Resources for Folkmanis Puppet catalog), bow ties (see Friend Crafts)

Directions: Introduce Tacky and talk with him about where he lives and what he likes to do. If a stuffed puppet is not available, make a stick puppet using the illustration in this story as a guideline. Use lots of dramatic expression when reading and you'll hear the children giggling as Tacky performs his antics. Ask the children to march in lines like the graceful penguins and then to march like Tacky. They will want to wear the paper or fabric bow ties while doing this.

de Beer, Hans. **LITTLE POLAR BEAR** (Holt, 1987).

Lars, a young polar bear, drifts out to sea while on a hunting trip with his father. He winds up in a jungle where he becomes friends with a hippopotamus who helps him find his way back to the North Pole. Other adventures about Lars includes LITTLE POLAR BEAR FINDS A FRIEND and AHOY THERE, LITTLE POLAR BEAR.

Dragonwagon, Crescent, il. by Ruth Bornstein. **YOUR OWL FRIEND** (Harper & Row, 1977).

An owl comes out of the dark to be a boy's friend. They explore together, running and flying through the night. The owl knows that the boy needs his love.

Dugan, Barbara, il. by James Stevenson. **LOOP THE LOOP** (Greenwillow, 1992).

Anne spends her days playing with her doll, Eleanor, until she becomes friends with Mrs. Simpson, a feisty old lady. Mrs. Simpson gradually becomes too old to care for herself and must enter a nursing home. Anne takes over the care of Mrs. Simpson's cat and gives her doll to Mrs. Simpson.

Dumbleton, Mike, il. by Ann James. **DIAL-A-CROC** (Orchard, 1991).

Vanessa goes to the outback and snares a crocodile. She gives the crocodile a choice. It can become purses and shoes, or it can help her make money. The two form the Dial-a-Croc business in which the croc performs various jobs, such as being the feature in a house of horrors. Then the crocodile gives Vanessa a choice. She can become breakfast, or she can take him home to the outback. She takes him home.

Ernst, Lisa Campbell. **WALTER'S TAIL** (Bradbury, 1992).

Old Mrs. Tully lives alone on the hill. She gets a puppy named Walter to keep her company and the two become good friends. Walter's tail constantly wags, and when he gets big, Walter wags an heroic rescue.

Graham, Margaret Bloy. **BENJY AND HIS FRIEND FIFI** (Harper & Row, 1988).

A lovable mutt named Benjy, and Fifi, a shy, nervous poodle, are good friends. When Fifi goes to her first dog show, Benjy goes along to keep her from getting nervous. At the dog show, all the noise and excitement put Fifi in a panic, but Benjy helps calm her down.

Gretz, Susanna. **FROG, DUCK AND RABBIT** (Four Winds, 1992).

Frog, Duck, and Rabbit work together to create a costume for a parade, but squabbling soon develops. When the parade is about to begin, they put their differences aside and make a prize-winning costume.

Heine, Helme. **FRIENDS** (Atheneum, 1982).

Charlie Rooster, Johnny Mouse, and Percy the Pig are very best friends who have fun together. They play hide and seek, pretend they're pirates, go fishing and pick cherries. However, they learn that even though they're best of friends, sometimes it's just not possible to do everything together.

Henkes, Kevin. **JESSICA** (Greenwillow, 1989).

Jessica is Ruthie's imaginary friend. Ruthie's parents want her to make some new friends when she goes to kindergarten. She does find a friend, and surprises

everyone when they discover her new friend's name is Jessica, too.

Hoban, Russell, il. by Lillian Hoban. **BEST FRIENDS FOR FRANCES** (Harper & Row, 1969).

The characters in this story are endearing badgers. Albert won't play ball with Frances because her little sister Gloria interferes by crying all the time. Albert thinks that Gloria is good for nothing. However, Frances convinces Albert of the value of her friendship, and Albert learns to appreciate Gloria.

Kellogg, Steven. **BEST FRIENDS** (Dial, 1986).

Kathy and Louise are best friends who do everything together. They share their chocolate milk and ride make-believe horses. When Louise moves away for the summer, Kathy feels lonely and betrayed. Then a new neighbor with a new-born puppy makes friends with Kathy as they care for the puppy together.

Kubler, Susanne. **THE THREE FRIENDS** (Macmillan, 1985).

Duffel the Bear and Sam the Hare enjoy listening to the many wonderful stories told by their friend Cat the Adventurer. When Duffel and Sam discover that Cat's stories are only make-believe, they learn to appreciate Cat as a storyteller.

Lester, Helen, il. by Lynn Munsinger. **A PORCUPINE NAMED FLUFFY** (Houghton Mifflin, 1986).

A little porcupine named Fluffy is not happy with his name. Then he meets a rhinoceros named Hippo and the two become the very best of friends.

MacLachlan, Patricia, il. by Tomie de Paola. **MOON, STARS, FROGS AND FRIENDS** (Pantheon, 1980).

Randall is a lonely frog who lives in a pond. One day, a frog prince appears in the pond. The two become friends and talk about the moon, stars, frogs, and friends. The frog prince turns back into a prince and marries Witch Esme. But the princess turns into a frog and marries Randall, so he isn't lonely any more.

Maestro, Betsy and Giulio. **WHERE IS MY FRIEND?** (Crown, 1976).

Harriet the elephant looks up and down, around, through, under, and over for her little mouse friend. She ends up finding the little mouse right in front of her nose.

Majewski, Joe, il. by Maria Majewski. **A FRIEND FOR OSCAR MOUSE** (Dial, 1988).

Oscar, a house mouse, ventures out into the country where he meets another mouse named Alfie. They become good companions. Together they play hide and seek, swing from the clothesline, jump from water lily to water lily, and run away from a hungry fox.

Marshall, James. **GEORGE AND MARTHA ROUND AND ROUND** (Houghton Mifflin, 1988).

George and Martha are two hippopotamuses who like to play jokes on each other. In the first chapter, Martha makes some unwanted comments about George's artistic abilities, so he lets Martha finish his picture. In the second chapter, George turns the sprinkler on Martha and tells her it is raining. Other books about these two friends include: GEORGE AND MARTHA, GEORGE AND MARTHA ENCORE.

Mayer, Mercer. **JUST MY FRIEND AND ME** (Western, 1988).

Little Critter wants a friend to climb trees,

play hide and seek and basketball, swing, and jump rope with. It's nice to have a friend, but sometimes it's nice to be alone, too.

McKissack, Patricia C., il. by Scott Cook. **NETTIE JO'S FRIENDS** (Knopf, 1989).

Nettie Jo won't go to her cousin's wedding unless she can take her favorite doll, Annie Mae. But Annie Mae needs a new dress and Nettie Jo can't find a needle to stitch the dress. She asks her animal friends to help, but they are busy with their own problems. However, they do find a needle for Nettie Jo to use.

Miller, Edna. **MOUSEKIN FINDS A FRIEND** (Prentice-Hall, 1967).

Mousekin sets out through the forest to find another creature like himself. Along the way, he encounters a fox-finch, a real fox, a turtle, a turtle dove, and a weasel before meeting another mouse.

Munsch, Robert, il. by Suzanne Duranceau. **MILLICENT AND THE WIND** (Firefly, 1984).

Millicent lives on a mountain far away from other children, and she longs for a friend to play with. The wind becomes her friend, and eventually carries to the mountains a boy who befriends Millicent.

Olsen, Ib Spang. **THE GROWN-UP TRAP** (Thomasson-Grant, 1992).

Caroline loves her parents, but they never seem to have enough time for her. So she decides to build a trap to catch her parents to make them spend time with her.

Ostheeren, Ingrid, il. by Agnes Mathieu. **JONATHAN MOUSE AND THE BABY BIRD** (North-South Books, 1991).

Jonathan is a mischievous little mouse, but when he finds a lost baby bird who has fallen out of its nest, he helps the bird by building it a soft nest, finding it a worm, and teaching it to fly.

Paige, Rob, il. by Paul Yalowitz. **SOME OF MY BEST FRIENDS ARE MONSTERS** (Bradbury, 1988).

A young boy's best friends are monsters who help him move the refrigerator, tie his shoes, and scare away a barking dog. He especially likes the monsters when they keep him company in the dark.

Pare, Roger. **A FRIEND LIKE YOU** (Annick, 1988).

Two cats share their lives as they dance, sing, go on a walk, ski, and read stories together. They're glad to be such good friends.

Polacco, Patricia. **CHICKEN SUNDAY** (Philomel, 1992).

Despite their differences in sex, race, and religion, two young boys are best friends with Patricia. Patricia even chooses the boys' grandmother as her own surrogate grandmother.

Samuels, Barbara. **DUNCAN & DOLORES** (Bradbury, 1986).

Dolores gets a new cat named Duncan. But Duncan doesn't like playing with Dolores. He doesn't want to play dress up or do tricks. Dolores decides to ignore Duncan, and that's when he decides he wants Dolores to be his friend after all.

Samuels, Barbara. **WHAT'S SO GREAT ABOUT CINDY SNAPPLEBY?** (Orchard, 1992).

Faye wants to be friends with snobby Cindy Snappleby. However, when Cindy

calls Faye's little sister a witch, Faye decides that it's more important to keep her sister as a friend than it is to be pals with Cindy.

Sharmat, Marjorie Weinman, il. by Tony DeLuna. **I'M NOT OSCAR'S FRIEND ANYMORE** (E. P. Dutton, 1975).

Oscar and his friend have a disagreement and aren't friends any more. Each thinks that the other will be unhappy without their friendship bond. Finally, the friend calls Oscar and they discover they are still friends despite their argument.

Stevenson, James. **NO FRIENDS** (Greenwillow, 1986).

Louie and Mary Ann have moved into a new neighborhood and complain to Grandpa that they don't have any friends. So Grandpa tells the story of how he and his little brother made friends in a new place, and before long some new friends come to visit. Together they go out for ice cream.

Vincent, Gabrielle. **FEEL BETTER, ERNEST** (Greenwillow, 1988).

Celestine the mouse takes very good care of her friend Ernest the bear when he becomes ill and must stay in bed. When Ernest gets bored, Celestine entertains him. Soon Ernest is well again and they celebrate his recovery by having a superb dinner together.

Wagener, Gerda, il. by Reinhard Michl. **LEO THE LION** (HarperCollins, 1991).

Lovable Leo the lion longs for a friend who will pet and care for him, but everyone he asks to be his friend is frightened away by his size. Leo goes on a long trip where he finds a lioness who strokes his mane, and Leo isn't lonely any longer.

Wilhelm, Hans. **LET'S BE FRIENDS AGAIN!** (Crown, 1986).

A boy's little sister sets his pet turtle free when she thinks the turtle needs more exercise. The boy is extremely angry and has trouble controlling his temper. However, as time passes, he's able to overcome his anger and forgives his sister. The two go together to the pet shop and buy a pair of hamsters.

Williams, Joyce. **BENTLY & EGG** (Harper/Collins, 1992).

Bently, a musical frog, baby-sits his duck friend Kack Kack's egg. The fun begins when a child steals the egg and Bently must rescue it.

Winthrop, Elizabeth, il. by Martha Weston. **THE BEST FRIENDS CLUB: A LIZZIE AND HAROLD STORY** (Lothrop, Lee & Shepard, 1989).

Lizzie and Harold decide to form a Best Friends Club with only two members. All is fine until Lizzie makes a lot of rules that Harold doesn't like. They decide that it's best to share friends to remain true friends.

Wolkstein, Diane, il. by Mary Jane Begin. **LITTLE MOUSE'S PAINTING** (Morrow, 1992).

Little Mouse enjoys visiting her friends Bear, Squirrel, and Porcupine. However, one day she devotes her time to painting instead. When the animals interpret the picture, they see themselves in the painting.

Zolotow, Charlotte, il. by James Stevenson. **I KNOW A LADY** (Puffin, 1986).

Sally knows a loving and lovable old lady who lives in her neighborhood. The lady gives children candied apples on Halloween and invites them in for cookies at Christmas time. She always waves to the children as they walk by her home and they love her a lot.

Friend Poems and Finger Plays

Read a poem to a friend!

CROSS PATCH

Cross Patch, draw the latch,
Sit by the fire and spin.
Take a cup and drink it up,
Then call your neighbors in.
—Mother Goose

CURLY LOCKS

Curly Locks, Curly Locks,
Wilt thou be mine?
Thou shalt not wash dishes
Nor yet feed the swine,
But sit on a cushion
And sew a fine seam,
And feed upon strawberries,
Sugar, and cream.
—Mother Goose

LITTLE CLOTILDA

Little Clotilda,
Well and hearty,
Thought she'd like
To give a party.
But as her friends
Were shy and wary,
Nobody came
But her own canary.
—Anonymous

HANDS

This hand can wave.
(Wave one hand keeping the other
    behind back.)
And its fingers can snap.
(Snap fingers.)
But it needs a friend
(Bring out the other hand.)
When it wants to clap.
(Clap hands together.)

"HELLO"
(Begin the day with this rhyme.)

"Hello" to my friends today,
I'm happy as can be.
You're very special friends,
And I'm glad you like me.
(Point to friends around room and then
    to self.)

More Friend Poems and Finger Plays

"Hug O'War," p. 19 and "Two Boxes," p. 41, in WHERE THE SIDEWALK ENDS by Shel Silverstein (Harper & Row, 1974).

"My Teddy Bear," p. 53, in READ-ALOUD RHYMES FOR THE VERY YOUNG selected by Jack Prelutsky, il. by Marc Brown (Knopf, 1986).

"Friendship," p. 108, in A NEW TREASURY OF CHILDREN'S POETRY selected by Joanna Cole, il. by Judith Gwyn Brown (Doubleday, 1984).

BEST FRIENDS, selected by Lee Bennett Hopkins, il. by James Watts (Harper & Row, 1986).

"Two Little Friends," p. 98, "Friends," p. 33, and "New Friends," p. 66, in RING A RING O'ROSES: FINGER PLAYS FOR PRE-SCHOOL CHILDREN (Flint Public Library, 1988).

SPECIAL FRIENDS
(Tune: "Oh, Do You Know the Muffin-Man?")

Oh! Do you know a special friend?
A special friend, a special friend?
   Oh! Do you know a special friend
Who wants to play with me?
(Look around at friends and point to
   self.)

Yes, I am your special friend,
A special friend, a special friend.
Yes, I am your special friend
Who likes to play with you.
(Hold hands with a friend.)

Oh! Do you know my other friends?
My other friends, my other friends?
Oh! Do you know my other friends
Who want to play with us?
(Point to other friends.)

Oh! Yes, we are the best of friends,
The best of friends, the best of friends.
Oh! Yes, we are the best of friends
Who love to run and play.
(All join hands and walk around.)

THE MORE WE GET TOGETHER

The more we get together, together,
   together,
The more we get together, the happier
   we'll be.
For your friends are my friends,
And my friends are your friends.
The more we get together, the happier
   we'll be.

The more we play together, together,
   together,

The more we play together, the happier
   we'll be.
For my toys are your toys,
And your books are my books.
The more we play together, the happier
   we'll be.

The more we work together, together,
   together,
The more we work together, the happier
   we'll be.
For my chores are your chores,
And your work is my work.
The more we work together, the happier
   we'll be.
—Adapted by Maxine Riggers

(First verse: Point fingers at friends, then
to self. Second verse: Join hands and
dance around. Third verse: Shake hands
with everyone.)

More Friend Songs

"Bow Belinda," p. 8 and "Buddies and
Pals," p. 10, in DO YOUR EARS HANG
LOW? (Fifty More Musical Finger Plays)
by Tom Glazer, il. by Mila Lazarevich
(Doubleday, 1980).

Friend Dramatic Play

GEORGE AND MARTHA

Provide dress-up clothes similar to what George and Martha wear, and let the children reenact some of the twosome's adventures. Tape a rope to the floor and let the children try walking the rope while holding an umbrella.

FOLLOW A FRIEND

Pair children off to play a version of the game "Follow the Leader." They should take turns being the leader and the follower. Suggest these actions to get the friends started: jump, stamp, skip, hop on one foot, tip-toe, jog in place, or dance.

MAY I BRING A FRIEND DRAMATIZATION

Props: six different stuffed animals, play dishes, food, an invitation in an envelope

Characters: king, queen, little boy

Let someone retell the story while the characters act it out using the props. To involve more children, let them play the various animals instead of using toys. Props are fun, but not necessary.

LET'S BE FRIENDS CHANT
(Do what the words indicate, keeping up the momentum.)

Let's be friends and all join hands,
And around and around we go.
Clap, clap, clap your hands,
And touch your toes.
Join those hands again,
And this time count to ten.
1, 2, 3, 4, 5, 6, 7, 8, 9, 10.
Now it's time to rest a bit,
And find a place to sit.

FABULOUS FRIEND PUPPET

Materials: three-inch Styrofoam ball, man's athletic tube sock, empty soup-size tin can, felt scraps, movable eyes, tacky glue, 14" dowel stick, curly ribbon, scissors

Directions: Push the dowel stick into the Styrofoam ball about 1" and glue it in place. Insert the ball into the toe of the sock. Remove both ends of the can and discard; clean the can. Insert the can into the sock just far enough to be held in place. Glue felt facial features and curly ribbon hair in place to make the puppet's head. To play with the puppet, hold onto the can with one hand and move the stick with the other. The head will twist around and move up and down.

GREEK FISHERMAN'S CAP

Materials: cap pattern, lightweight black poster paper, blue tissue paper, gold-colored yarn, scissors, stapler, glue

Directions: Use the pattern provided to cut out the bill of the cap from black paper. Cut a strip 1 1/2" by 25" for rim of cap. Staple together to fit head. Cut slits about 1/2" deep along the inner edge of the bill, fold down, and staple to the rim. Cut a 10" to 12" circle from blue tissue paper. Glue to the inside of the rim, gathering as you go to make the crown of the hat. Braid yarn and glue across the bill. Make this cap after reading FOX AND HEGGIE. Refer to the Read-Aloud section for additional ideas.

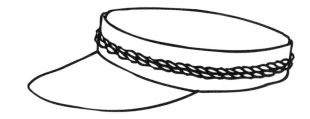

TACKY'S BOW TIE

Materials: fabric scraps or tissue paper, stapler, big safety pins, scissors

Directions: Cut fabric into strips about 4" by 12". Fold lengthwise, bringing the unfinished edges together in the middle. Bring the short ends together in the middle so they overlap. Staple together. Cut a smaller piece of fabric to wrap around the middle of the strip, gathering in to make a bow. Staple the ends of the smaller piece together. Attach to clothing with a large safety pin. Make bow ties after reading TACKY THE PENGUIN. Refer to the Read-Aloud section for additional ideas.

PAPER DOLL FRIENDS

Materials: girl and boy patterns, long sheets of easily folded colored paper, scissors, pencil

Directions: Fold paper accordion-style the width of the doll pattern so the arms will touch each side (see pattern for easy to understand pictorial directions). Trace the pattern onto the top of the folded paper, and cut out, leaving the arms attached. Unfold and open the paper. The dolls will be holding hands. Pin the cutouts around a world globe or map to illustrate that we should be friendly with people around the world.

FRIENDSHIP CIRCLE

Materials: butcher paper, pencil, scissors, markers or crayons, tape

Directions: Provide enough butcher paper for each child to make a life-size self-portrait. Pair up the children, and have them take turns lying on the paper with arms spread out while the other child traces around them. Each child should draw features and clothes onto his or her own self-portrait. Cut out and tape up the likenesses around the room as if the pictures are holding hands.

Fabulous Friend Puppet

1. Glue dowel stick in Styrofoam ball.

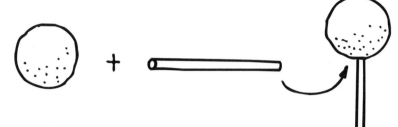

2. Insert ball into sock and glue on facial features.

3. Insert can into sock.

Facial Feature Patterns
Cut from felt

Mouth and eyebrows
Cut one for mouth and
two for eyebrows.

Eyes
Cut two.

Cap Pattern

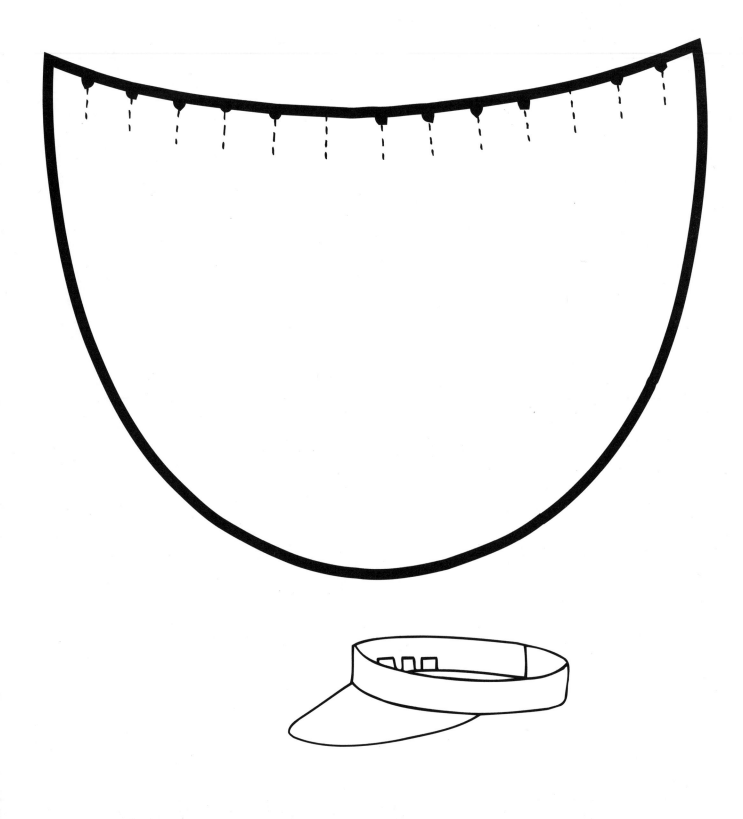

Girl and Boy Patterns

65

Friend Snacks

Encourage the children to share a snack with a friend—divide a Popsicle, share a box of animal crackers, or sip a glass of milk with two straws. After reading NO FRIENDS by Janet Stevenson, the children may want to have ice cream cones together.

FRIENDSHIP GORP

(Serves 10)

1 cup peanuts
1 cup chocolate candies
1 cup raisins
1 cup corn cereal squares

Combine the ingredients in a paper bag and shake lightly to mix. Then have the children share this nutritious snack. Some children may want to make the mix at home to take hiking with a friend.

FRIENDSHIP COOKIES

Make your favorite rolled sugar cookie recipe and cut out the rolled dough with a round cookie or biscuit cutter. Cut paper straws into short pieces and insert one into each cookie before baking. When the cookies have cooled, remove the straws and let the children decorate the cookies, making funny faces. Tie ribbons through the holes and hang the cookies on a friendship tree (a sturdy potted plant). Encourage the children to guess who made each cookie. Let friends exchange cookies if they wish.

SUB SANDWICHES

Set out baguettes halved lengthwise and a variety of meats, cheeses, vegetables, and condiments and let the children work together in groups to make long sub sandwiches. Cut the sandwiches into equal portions and invite the children to enjoy their cooperatively made snack.

Take time to taste lots of good books with the children—and lots of good food. Try unusual recipes using foods not usually found in your area. For instance, if you live in the north, try tropical fruits (papaya or mango), grits, or dishes from foreign countries.

Have a snack in an unusual place. Let the children experience eating while sitting in a tree or under a table. Take a field trip to an orchard, a vegetable garden, a bakery, a restaurant, or even the school cafeteria. The children will enjoy snapping green beans, eating olives from their fingers, making wishes on wishbones (around Thanksgiving time), and feeding bread crumbs to the birds.

Ask the children this riddle: "What is the best thing to put into a chocolate cake?" "Your teeth." They'll also enjoy saying this verse: "Over the teeth, past the gums, look out stomach, here it comes."

SETTING THE STAGE

In the reading corner, put all the books about food in a picnic basket or shopping cart (real or play). Wear a chef's hat or an apron while telling stories. The children will want to try these on while playing in the housekeeping area or reading about food.

Make gigantic paper food cutouts as illustrated in CLOUDY WITH A CHANCE OF MEATBALLS by Judi Barrett to cover the walls. Cut out pictures of food from magazines and glue onto oaktag to hang from the ceiling with string.

Set up a supermarket with empty food boxes covered in Contact paper, a cash register with play money, and paper sacks (don't use plastic). Limit the play area to a few children at a time.

BULLETIN BOARD IDEAS

1. Enlarge and copy the "Picnic with Books" illustration. Color, cut out, and mat if desired. For a three-dimensional effect, use fabric for the picnic cloth and book covers for the books.

2. After reading RECHENKA'S EGGS by Patricia Polacco, have the children draw, cut out, and decorate paper eggs. Display as a collage.

3. Have a "Bookfeast!" On a large sheet of paper, create a menu of books about food that the children can choose from. Title it "Gourmet Book Menu."

4. Make a big cone and several scoops of ice cream from different colors of construction paper. Pin up the cone. Add a scoop to the cone each time a book about food is read. Print the title of the book on the scoop. This may be done as a class project, or individually for children who can read. You might also make a gigantic ice cream cone to display on the wall or door.

5. Purchase and display an "In the Night Kitchen" poster, available at bookstores and poster shops.

Picnic with Books

BREAD AND JAM FOR FRANCES
by Russell Hoban, il. by Lillian Hoban (Harper & Row, 1964).

Story: Frances, a little badger, doesn't want to eat what the other members of the family eat for breakfast, lunch, and dinner. She wants to eat bread and jam. Mother and Father are very understanding, and provide her with an ample supply of bread and jam. Then Frances changes her mind and decides that it's best to eat other food, too.

Materials: bread, jam, table knives, napkins, milk

Directions: As you read the story, sing each verse that Frances sings. Create your own simple tune. Repeat the verse, asking the children to join in. Because the text is rather lengthy for young children, you may want to paraphrase or tell the story. However, be careful not to leave out any essential elements. After hearing the story, the children will be hungry for some of Frances' bread and jam. Let the children make their own. Serve with milk.

THE CAKE THAT MACK ATE
by Rose Robart, il. by Maryann Kovalski (Little, 1987).

Story: This cumulative verse begins with the egg that goes into the cake that Mack, the dog, ate. The egg is laid by the hen who ate the corn that grew from seeds, and so on, leading up to the making of the cake.

Materials: birthday cake

Directions: This is an ideal story to read on a child's birthday. The children will enjoy repeating the verse with you as the story progresses. Have a cake already baked and explain that Mack didn't eat this cake, he left it for everyone to enjoy.

CLOUDY WITH A CHANCE OF MEATBALLS
by Judi Barrett, il. by Ron Barrett
(Aladdin Books, 1978).

Story: In the village of Chewandswallow, there are no grocery stores, all the food the villagers need falls from the sky. Suddenly, things change. There's too much food, and the food is gigantic. A disaster develops, and the villagers must move to a town where food is sold in stores.

Materials: bread houses (see Food Crafts), instant mashed potatoes and butter, grapes, Jell-O mold

Directions: Give each child a few seedless grapes to toss into his or her mouth as if falling from the sky. Mix up a bowl of instant mashed potatoes with a pat of butter on the top and serve. You might consider making a Jell-O mold. Illustrations of both of these are in the book. Refer to Setting the Stage for additional ideas.

THE DOORBELL RANG
by Pat Hutchins (Scholastic, 1986).

Story: Ma makes a dozen cookies for tea and Victoria and Sam plan to share them equally. The cookies are good, but Ma keeps saying that Grandma makes the best cookies. The doorbell begins to ring, and each time more visitors arrive. When the children begin to worry there won't be enough cookies for all the guests, Grandma arrives with a big tray of cookies.

Materials: Grandma's cookies, bell

Directions: While reading the story, the children will enjoy repeating the refrain "No one makes cookies like Grandma." Ring a bell each time the doorbell rings in the story. At the end of the story, have a tray of cookies for the children to share. The children can help you make them ahead of time, or a grandma can assist in the baking, or a grandma might want to bring in a tray of cookies herself. The story provides an excellent opportunity for a math lesson: If two children divide the cookies, how many would each child have?

POPCORN
by Frank Asch (Parents Magazine Press, 1979).

Story: On Halloween night, when Sam Bear's parents are out, he invites his friends to an impromptu party. Soon, his house is filled with popcorn. When Sam's parents return, they bring a special treat for him—popcorn.

Materials: popcorn, hot air popcorn popper, stuffed toy bear wearing Indian costume similar to Sam's in the story

Directions: Introduce Sam to the children. If your Sam is a puppet, let the puppet talk to the children. Keep Sam in the room for the children to play with, or put him on the shelf as a reminder of the story. Pop popcorn and let the children eat it for a special snack.

THE POPCORN DRAGON
by Jane Thayer, il. by Jay Hyde Barnum (Morrow, 1953).

Story: Dexter, a young dragon, learns how to blow smoke. He enjoys showing off for his friends, but they become envious and decide not to play with him until Dexter accidentally discovers he can pop popcorn with his smoke. He treats his friends to a popcorn snack, and they forgive him for being a show-off.

Materials: popcorn, hot air popcorn popper, poster paper, glue

Directions: Pop a bowl of popcorn for the children to share. Talk about what makes the corn pop, where popcorn comes from, and what popcorn tastes like. Give a handful of corn to each child to count, then have them glue the popcorn onto paper to make a picture. Role play the story, letting some children pretend to be the dragon blowing smoke, while others play the popcorn pieces that pop. Have the children change places so that each child plays both parts.

PUMPKIN, PUMPKIN
by Jeanne Titherington (Greenwillow, 1985).

Story: Jamie plants a pumpkin seed in the spring. He watches it grow from a tiny sprout to a huge, orange pumpkin. On Halloween, the pumpkin's ready to pick and carve, but Jamie saves six seeds to plant the next spring. Also available as a Big Book.

Materials: pumpkins, carving knife, soil and container

Directions: Show a few pumpkin seeds to the children before reading the story. Demonstrate how to carve a pumpkin into a jack-o'-lantern. Let the children watch, and emphasize that adult supervision is needed when using a knife. Let some of the seeds dry, then plant them in soil and have the children watch them grow. The seedlings should be transplanted into a garden to finish growing. Roast the remaining seeds (see Food Snacks).

STONE SOUP
by Marcia Brown (Scribner's, 1947).

Story: A tired, hungry soldier convinces an old lady he can make soup from a stone. The soldier adds the stone to the boiling water and asks the old woman to add onions, carrots, beef bones, salt, pepper, barley, and butter. The soup is delicious, and the two sit down together to a fine dinner of stone soup.

Materials: pot, stone, ingredients for soup, bowls, spoons, napkins

Directions: There are several repetitive refrains in this version of the popular fairy tale, and the children will want to repeat the phrases along with you. Read other versions of this tale to note and enjoy the differences. Make stone soup. Ask each child to bring a vegetable to put in the pot. Don't forget to include a scrubbed stone. Invite the school principal or parents to enjoy the soup with the students. Or let the children role play the story with an empty pot, spoon, and play food in the housekeeping corner. If play food is not available, the children can make their own from colored paper.

Andersen, Hans Christian, adapted by Jan Wahl, il. by Ray Cruz. **THE WOMAN WITH THE EGGS** (Crown, 1974).

On the way to market with her basket of eggs on her head, a greedy old woman dreams of the riches the eggs will bring to her. She imagines that she will be a grand lady, and when she tosses her head to show her greatness, all the eggs fall and break.

Burningham, John. **THE SHOPPING BASKET** (Crowell, 1980).

Steven takes the shopping basket to the store to purchase six eggs, five bananas, four apples, three oranges, two dough-nuts, and a package of crisps. On the way home, the boy outsmarts several intruders who want to eat the contents of his basket.

Cushman, Doug. **POSSUM STEW** (E. P. Dutton, 1990).

Possum is up to his old tricks again. He causes Bear and Gator to fall into the river so he can grab their basket of fish, which he eats for dinner. But Bear and Gator get back at Possum when they tell him they are going to make possum stew.

Degen, Bruce. **JAMBERRY** (Harper & Row, 1983).

A little boy wanders into the forest where he finds an endearing bear who takes him on a delicious berry-picking trip. Their adventure is told in rhyme as they pick blueberries, strawberries, black-berries, and more.

de Paola, Tomie. **TONY'S BREAD** (G. P. Putnam's Sons, 1989).

In this Italian folk tale, Tony's dream comes true when a nobleman helps him get his own bakery. Tony learns to make a unique loaf of bread, panetone, baked in a flower pot. In return the nobleman marries Tony's daughter. PANCAKES FOR BREAKFAST is another good book by this author.

de Paola, Tomie. **WATCH OUT FOR THE CHICKEN FEET IN YOUR SOUP** (Prentice-Hall, 1974).

Joey is embarrassed to introduce his friend Eugene to his old-fashioned Italian grandmother, but they end up having a wonderful time while visiting her and eating her chicken soup. Joey gains a new appreciation of his grandmother. There is a recipe for Bread Dolls at the end of the book.

Dunbar, Joyce, il. by Emilie Boon. **A CAKE FOR BARNEY** (Watts, 1988).

Barney, a bear, has a delicious cupcake with five cherries on it, but every time he decides to eat it someone comes along who wants a part. Barney gives away the five cherries, but when a bigger bear demands the cupcake, Barney gulps it down.

Ehlert, Lois. **GROWING VEGETABLE SOUP** (Harcourt Brace, 1987).

A father and his child plant, water, and watch seeds grow in their family garden. Then the corn, cabbage, potatoes, toma-toes, and other vegetables are cooked to make the best vegetable soup ever.

Gelman, Rita. **MORE SPAGHETTI, I SAY!** (Scholastic, 1977).

Minnie, a monkey, doesn't have time to play with Freddy, another monkey, because Minnie's always eating spa-ghetti. But when Minnie is finally full of spaghetti and wants to play, Freddy de-cides he also likes eating spaghetti and doesn't have time to play with Minnie.

Greeson, Janet, il. by David LaRochelle. **THE STINGY BAKER** (Carolrhoda, 1990).

This tale is the origin of the expression "a baker's dozen." A stingy baker refuses to give a mysterious old woman 13 cookies to the dozen instead of 12. The baker's business suffers misfortunes until he learns that generosity is better than greed. Another version of the same tale is THE BAKER'S DOZEN retold by Heather Forest.

Hale, Lucretia, adapt. and il. by Amy Schwartz. **THE LADY WHO PUT SALT IN HER COFFEE** (Harcourt Brace, 1989).

Mrs. Peterkin accidentally puts salt instead of sugar in her coffee. She can't drink it, so she calls in her family, who call in the chemist and the herb woman, who are unsuccessful in making the coffee drinkable again. Then a sensible lady from Philadelphia suggests making a fresh cup.

Hennessy, B. G., il. by Mary Morgan. **JAKE BAKED THE CAKE** (Scholastic, 1990).

There's going to be a wedding and Jake is making the cake. The wedding preparations are in full swing, Sally brings the rice, the groom's pants arrive from France, and Jake bakes a beautiful wedding cake.

Hennessy, B. G., il. by Tracey Campbell Pearson. **THE MISSING TARTS** (Viking Kestrel, 1989).

When the Queen of Tarts' strawberry tarts are stolen by the Knave of Hearts, she enlists the help of nursery rhyme characters Jack and Jill, Old Mother Hubbard, Jack Sprat, and others to get the tarts back. Eventually, the Queen discovers that the Knave has given the tarts to the children of the Old Woman Who Lives in a Shoe.

Howe, James, il. by Leslie Morrill. **HOT FUDGE** (Morrow, 1990).

This story is told by a dog, Harold, who loves fudge. Harold lives with the Monroe family, who are always making chewy, chocolatey, melt-in-your mouth fudge. A special batch of fudge disappears and Harold helps find the fudge thief.

Hutchins, Pat. **DON'T FORGET THE BACON** (Puffin, 1986).

Mother sends her young boy off to town to purchase eggs, a cake, pears, and bacon. The boy thinks that the best way to remember the shopping list is to repeat it, but instead he gets confused and forgets the bacon.

Joosse, Barbara, il. by Emily Arnold McCully. **JAM DAY** (Harper & Row, 1987).

Ben and his mother ride the train to his grandparents to join all the family in their annual family reunion. They spend the day picking strawberries to make strawberry jam. Grandpa makes his famous biscuits to go with the jam, and the big, noisy family has a great time together.

Kasza, Keiko. **THE WOLF'S CHICKEN STEW** (G. P. Putnam's Sons, 1987).

A wolf attempts to fatten up a chicken he wants to put in his stew by feeding it a hundred pancakes, a hundred doughnuts, and a scrumptious cake. The wolf changes his mind when he visits Mrs. Chicken to capture her, and a batch of little chicks give him a hundred kisses for all the food he has brought them.

Kelley, True. **LET'S EAT** (E. P. Dutton, 1989).

This book presents illustrations about food: where it comes from, proper

etiquette, eating places, holiday treats, and even some good food tricks.

Littledale, Freya, il. by Molly Delaney. **THE FARMER IN THE SOUP** (Scholastic, 1987).

The farmer always complains that his wife never cooks what he wants. If he wants pie, she bakes cookies. The two decide to trade jobs and, through a series of disastrous events, the farmer ends up sitting in the pot of onion soup. Needless to say, the farmer never complains again.

Lord, John Vernon. **THE GIANT JAM SANDWICH** (Houghton Mifflin, 1972).

Four million wasps fly into Itching Down and begin pestering the villagers. The villagers get together to make a strawberry jam sandwich to trap the wasps. The birds carry the sandwich away in a large tablecloth, and the town of Itching Down is never bothered by wasps again.

Marshall, James. **YUMMERS!** (Houghton Mifflin, 1972).

Emily, a pig, decides to go walking for exercise and to lose weight. However, she's tempted by every yummy food she finds along the way. You'll also enjoy reading YUMMERS TOO, THE SECOND COURSE.

McCloskey, Robert. **BLUEBERRIES FOR SAL** (Viking, 1948).

Sal and her mother go to Blueberry Hill to pick berries. On the hill, Sal and her mother meet a mother bear and cub. The encounter is friendly, and the two pairs are able to pick all the blueberries they want.

McDonald, Megan, il. by Ted Lewin. **THE POTATO MAN** (Orchard, 1991).

The potato man drives his loaded cart down the street to sell potatoes. A group of children pester him and filch the potatoes that bounce off the cart. Later, a red pomegranate falls off the cart and the boys return it, but the potato man tells them to keep it and wishes them a merry Christmas.

Modell, Frank. **ICE CREAM SOUP** (Greenwillow, 1988).

Marvin and Milton decide to give themselves a birthday party. They send out invitations and make party hats, but their cake is flat and burned and the ice cream looks like soup. Their party looks like it will be a disaster until their friendly shopkeepers deliver a big, delicious cake and frozen ice cream.

Murphy, Jill. **A PIECE OF CAKE** (G. P. Putnam's Sons, 1989).

Mrs. Large, the mama elephant, decides her family must go on a diet. They eat watercress soup, grated carrots, and fish, and they get lots of exercise. However, when Granny sends them a cake, the diet is over.

Numeroff, Laura Joffe, il. by Felicia Bond. **IF YOU GIVE A MOOSE A MUFFIN** (HarperCollins, 1991).

When a little boy gives a hungry moose a muffin, the moose wants some jam to go with it. When he's eaten the muffin, he wants to go to the store to get more, and so goes the hilarious sequence of events which lead back to the boy giving the moose another muffin. IF YOU GIVE A MOUSE A COOKIE is another good book by the same author.

Pillar, Marjorie. **PIZZA MAN** (Crowell, 1990).

The Pizza Man begins his work by mixing flour, water, and yeast to make the

dough. He cooks the tomato sauce, adds the toppings, and the pizza is ready to serve to his hungry customers.

Polacco, Patricia. **RECHENKA'S EGGS** (Philomel, 1988).

Old Babushka is busy preparing her beautifully painted eggs for the festival. However, when she brings an injured goose into her house to care for, the goose accidentally overturns the basket of eggs, breaking them all. A miracle happens when Rechenka, the goose, lays beautiful painted eggs.

Polacco, Patricia. **THUNDER CAKE** (Philomel, 1990).

An impending thunderstorm frightens Grandma's little granddaughter, so the two gather ingredients to make a thunder cake. The child's fears of the thunderstorm are dispelled because they're busy making the cake. The recipe for "Grandma's Thunder Cake" is included at the end of the book.

Redhead, Janet Slater, il. by Christine Dale. **THE BIG BLOCK OF CHOCOLATE** (Ashton Scholastic, 1985).

Jenny buys a big block of chocolate, but puts it on the shelf to enjoy later. Her dog, cat, and a magpie each find the chocolate, but also decide to eat it later. Then the sun finds the chocolate, it melts, and a colony of ants enjoy the chocolate.

Rice, Eve. **BENNY BAKES A CAKE** (Greenwillow, 1981).

It's Benny's birthday, and he helps his mother bake a lovely birthday cake. However, Ralph, their dog, decides to help himself to the cake. The day is saved when Papa brings home another cake.

Sendak, Maurice. **IN THE NIGHT KITCHEN** (Harper & Row, 1970).

In this imaginative book, a small boy named Mickey dreams he falls through the dark and lands in the night kitchen, where he helps the bakers make the morning cake.

Seuss, Dr. **GREEN EGGS AND HAM** (Random House, 1960).

Sam tries everything to get his friend to eat green eggs and ham. In rhyme, he asks his friend to try them in a house or with a mouse, but it's not until Sam promises not to bother his friend any more that the friend decides to try them. Much to his surprise, he likes them.

Sharmart, Mitchell, il. by Jose Aruego and Ariane Dewey. **GREGORY THE TERRIBLE EATER** (Four Winds Press, 1980).

Gregory, a goat, is a very picky eater. He refuses to eat shoes, coats, and tin cans. He wants scrambled eggs, orange juice, vegetables, and fruit. Gregory's parents try to teach him to eat right, but discover it's best to let him eat whatever he wants.

Snow, Pegeen, il. by Mike Venezia. **EAT YOUR PEAS, LOUISE** (Children's Press, 1985).

Louise is given all sorts of reasons why she should eat her peas, but none of them convinces her until she hears the word "please."

Vaughan, Marica K., il. by Pamela Lofts. **WOMBAT STEW** (Ashton Scholastic, 1984).

On the banks of the Billabong, a very clever dingo (wild dog) catches a fat wombat to use to make a yummy stew.

WHO EVER SAUSAGE A THING?

One day a boy went walking
And went into a store;
He bought a pound of sausages
And laid them on the floor.
The boy began to whistle
A merry little tune—
And all the little sausages
Danced around the room!
—Anonymous

MY FATHER OWNS THE BUTCHER SHOP

My father owns the butcher shop,
My mother cuts the meat,
And I'm the little hot dog
That runs around the street.
—Anonymous

I EAT MY PEAS WITH HONEY

I eat my peas with honey;
I've done it all my life.
It makes the peas taste funny,
But it keeps them on the knife.
—Author Unknown

THE SLOPPY GENTLEMAN

There was a sloppy gentleman
Who loved to eat all day.
He spilled spaghetti and meatballs
In every which way.
His pretty tablecloth was white
When he began to eat.
But quickly changed to stripes and dots
For he was not too neat!
—Unknown

Mother Goose Rhymes:

WHEN JACK'S A VERY GOOD BOY

When Jack's a very good boy,
He shall have cakes and custard;
But when he does nothing but cry,
He shall have nothing but mustard.

HANDY-SPANDY

Handy-spandy,
Jack-a-dandy,
Loves plum cake
And sugar candy.
He bought some
At a grocer's shop,
And out he came
Hop, hop, hop, hop.

LITTLE TOMMY TUCKER

Little Tommy Tucker
Sings for his supper.
What shall we give him?
White bread and butter.
How shall he cut it
Without any knife?
How shall he marry
Without any wife?

LITTLE JACK HORNER

Little Jack Horner
Sat in a corner,
Eating a Christmas Pie.
He put in his thumb
And pulled out a plum,
And said, "What a good boy am I."

BETTY BOTTER

Betty Botter bought some butter,
But, she said, the butter's bitter;
If I put it in my batter,
It will make my batter bitter,
But a bit of better butter
Will make my batter better.
So she bought a bit a butter
Better than her bitter butter,
And she put it in her batter
And the batter was not bitter.
So it was better Betty Botter bought
A bit a better butter.

Food Finger Plays & Action Verses

PIZZA, PIZZA

Pizza, pizza
Pepperoni pizza,
I could eat pizza (Pretend to eat.)
All day long. (Rub stomach.)
Hot dogs, hot dogs
Covered in ketchup. (Lick lips.)
I could eat hot dogs
All day long. (Rub stomach.)
Popcorn, popcorn,
Hot, buttery popcorn. (Jump up and
    down.)
I could eat popcorn
All day long. (Rub stomach.)
Ice cream, ice cream
Peanut butter ice cream. (Lick ice
    cream cone.)
I could eat ice cream
All day long. (Rub stomach.)
Pizza, pizza, (Pretend to eat.)
Hot dogs, hot dogs, (Lick lips.)
Popcorn, popcorn, (Jump up and
    down.)
Ice cream, ice cream, (Lick a cone.)
I could eat good food
All day long. (Rub stomach.)

Encourage children to create their own
verses and actions.

TEN ORANGES ON A TREE

Ten round oranges on a tree, (Hold
    fingers up high.)
Five for you and five for me. (Wiggle
    fingers on each hand.)
When you shake the tree just so, (Shake
    body.)
Ten round oranges will fall below. (Lower
    hands.)
1, 2, 3, 4, 5, 6, 7, 8, 9, 10. (Count on
    fingers.)

Encourage the children to create other
verses about other fruit trees.

PEAS PORRIDGE HOT

Peas porridge hot,
Peas porridge cold,
Peas porridge in the pot,
Nine days old.
Some like it hot.
Some like it cold.
And some like it in the pot,
Nine days old
—Traditional

As the children chant, have them sit in
pairs on the floor facing each other. Let
them clap hands on legs, clap hands
together, and clap hands with other
person, palms together.

More Food Finger Plays and Action Verses

"Cooking and Eating," pp. 82- 92, in
MOVE OVER MOTHER GOOSE by Ruth L.
Dowell, il. by Concetta C. Scott
(Gryphon House, 1987).

"The Bakery," p. 6, "A Churning We Will
Go," p. 13, "The Cows" and "Cup of
Tea," p. 16, "A Delicious Cake," p. 17,
"The Doughnut," p. 19, "Making
Cookies," p. 59, "Pancake," p. 71, "The
Pumpkin," p. 74, "What Am I Baking?", p.
102, and "Who Stole the Cookie from
the Cookie Jar?", p. 105, in RING A RING
O'ROSES: FINGER PLAYS FOR PRE-
SCHOOL CHILDREN (Flint Public Library,
1988).

POP, POP
(Tune: "London Bridge")

Pop, pop, pop, pop, pop, pop, pop,
Pop, pop, pop,
Pop, pop, pop.
Pop, pop, pop, pop, pop, pop, pop.
I love popcorn!

(Sing this song while popping popcorn.
Have the children sing it slowly the first
time while they pop up and down. Then
have them sing it again, faster and
faster each time.)

HOT CROSS BUNS!

Hot cross buns!
Hot cross buns!
One a penny, two a penny,
Hot cross buns!
Give them to your daughters.
Give them to your sons.
Hot cross buns!
Hot cross buns!
—Mother Goose

(Do these motions at the appropriate
place in the verse: slap your legs, cross
arms across chest, hold up one and
then two fingers, and repeat actions on
last two lines.)

POLLY, PUT THE KETTLE ON

Polly, put the kettle on,
Polly, put the kettle on,
Polly, put the kettle on,
We'll all have tea.
Sukey, take it off again,
Sukey, take it off again,
Sukey, take it off again,
They've all gone away.
—Mother Goose

OH, DO YOU KNOW THE MUFFIN-MAN?

Oh, do you know the muffin-man,
The muffin-man, the muffin-man?
Oh, do you know the muffin-man
Who lives in Drury Lane?
Yes, I know the muffin-man,
The muffin-man, the muffin-man.
Yes, I know the muffin-man
Who lives in Drury Lane!
—Mother Goose

(Have the children hold hands in a circle
and slowly walk around when singing.
Put one child in the center to be the
muffin man. Repeat with a different
child in the center, using the child's
name. For example, "Do you know
Cassidy Rose who lives on Whitman
Street?")

More Food Songs

"On Top of Spaghetti," p. 128, "I Scream,
You Scream, We All Scream for Ice
Cream," p. 143, and "Sing a Song of
Sixpence" p. 222, in READER'S DIGEST
CHILDREN'S SONG BOOK (Reader's
Digest General Books, 1985).

Food Games and Dramatic Play

BLUEBERRY HUNT

Before reading BLUEBERRIES FOR SAL, hide fresh blueberries (wrapped in small amounts in plastic wrap) in a designated area. Give the players a pail to share. When the berries have all been gathered, have a feast!

FOOD FUN

Have the children try these food antics: eat peas from Popsicle stick "knives" (you might have to add honey), balance a vegetable or piece of fruit on their nose (carrot, orange, grape), and pretend they're a bird eating worms (noodles).

A GIANT JAM SANDWICH

Divide the children into wasps, villagers, and birds. The wasps stand in a corner of the room and swarm out making a buzzing sound. Meanwhile, the villagers prepare the giant jam sandwich. The wasps land on the sandwich, the villagers slap a piece of bread on top of them, and the birds carry the sandwich away. Encourage the children to use their imaginations instead of props.

DON'T FORGET THE BACON

Make a game out of this story. The children sit in circles in small groups. One player whispers a phrase to the next child, who whispers it to the next, and so on around the circle. The last player repeats the phrase as he or she heard it. Of course it will be quite different by this point, so the first player should repeat the original phrase. Be prepared for lots of laughs!

PLACE MATS

Materials: colored construction paper (12" x 18" or 9" x 12"), scissors, paper scraps, glue

Directions: Give each child a sheet of paper and some paper scraps. Ask the children to cut out designs from the scraps and glue them onto the sheets of paper. Laminate so the mats may be used over and over. Put the place mats on the table for snack time and let the children find their own. Older children can weave a place mat. Cut slits in each sheet of paper leaving about one inch all the way around the edges. Cut strips of contrasting colored paper and let the children weave them in and out.

BREAD HOUSES
(Do this activity after reading CLOUDY WITH A CHANCE OF MEATBALLS.)

Materials: stale bread, hot-glue gun, knife

Directions: Have the children refer to the book illustrations for construction ideas. Purchase old bread reduced in price and spread it out to dry. Let the children cut windows, doors, and any special shapes they want in the bread before it gets too hard. Have adult volunteers use the hot-glue gun to glue the children's bread slices together in the house shape they want. Place all the houses together to make a village. It's best to have two children work together on one house.

RECHENKA'S EGGS

Materials: hard-boiled eggs, watercolor paints, brushes, needles

Directions: After reading this story, the children will be anxious to paint eggs like Babushka's. Encourage them to paint the entire egg and use lots of colors. Older children will want to paint un-cooked eggshells. Show them how to poke holes with a needle in both ends of an egg and blow out the insides. The eggshells will keep forever or until they're dropped. Refer to Bulletin Board Ideas for other suggestions.

There are a lot of options for snacks related to stories about food, but following are a few special ideas.

GREEN EGGS AND HAM

Break as many eggs as desired into a bowl. Let the children add a few drops of green food coloring and mix, then add small pieces of cooked ham and salt and pepper to taste. Cover the bottom of a skillet with cooking oil, pour in the egg mixture, and cook until done, stirring constantly. Once the children try these green eggs and ham, they'll discover they like them.

GINGERBREAD MEN

Use a gingerbread man cookie cutter to cut out shapes from bread. Let the children spread the shapes with peanut butter, decorate them with raisins, and gobble them up!

SIMPLE VEGGIE SOUP

Mix the following together in an electric skillet:
1 large can tomato soup
1 beef bouillon cube
package of mixed frozen vegetables

Bring to a boil and cook until heated through. Serve in small, heat-proof paper cups. Serves 6.

ROASTED PUMPKIN SEEDS

Remove the seeds from a pumpkin and boil them in salted water for about 10 minutes. Roast the seeds in the oven at 200 degrees for 10 to 15 minutes, or until light brown. Butter may be added to the roasting pan, but is not necessary.

BUTTER

Divide the children into groups of three. Give each group a small jar of cream (whipping cream will work) with a tight lid. Have the children take turns shaking the jar until it turns to butter (about 6 to 8 minutes). It will be soft. Refrigerate to harden if desired. Spread this yummy homemade butter on bread for all to enjoy.

There's a special love that spans generations—the love between grandchildren and grandparents. You can support this love by reading some of the wonderful books that focus on grandparents, and by holding a "Grandparent Week" in the library or classroom. Invite grandparents to read to the children or to tell their personal stories. Older children will enjoy sharing their reading skills with the guests.

You may also wish to have a "Steven Kellogg Week," and read only his books during that time. Kellogg has written a number of books in which a lovable grandfather tells very funny tall tales. Place the author's books in a basket and choose one to read each day.

SETTING THE STAGE

Place a child-sized rocking chair in the reading corner with a basket of books about grandparents sitting beside it. The reader should sit in the rocking chair while reading the books. You may also want to copy illustrations from some of the books to cut out and display in the reading corner.

BULLETIN BOARD IDEAS

1. Enlarge and copy the illustration "Going to see Grandma" onto poster paper using an opaque projector. Color the little girl's cape red. Make curls out of wrapping ribbon and glue on for the hair. In this story, Little Red Riding Hood's grandmother is well, so the little girl takes books in her basket when she visits for some enjoyable reading.

2. Title the bulletin board "Picture a Grandparent." Copy illustrations of grandparents from story books, and pin them up as the start of a collage. Ask the children to contribute by bringing in and pinning up photos of their own grandparents.

3. Enlarge, copy, and pin up any of the grandparent book covers. HAPPY BIRTHDAY, SAM by Pat Hutchins is a good choice. Use a real balloon and sailboat for a three-dimensional effect.

Bulletin Board

COCO CAN'T WAIT

by Taro Gomi (Morrow, 1984).

Story: Coco goes to visit her grandmother, and on the same day Grandma packs apples in a basket and decides to visit Coco. They miss each other along the way. The two go back and forth several times until they finally meet under the apple tree where they enjoy eating Grandma's apples.

Materials: basket of yellow apples, Grandma and Coco finger puppets (see Grandparent Crafts)

Directions: Bring out the basket of Grandma's apples and explain that she's taking the apples to her granddaughter. Read the story, letting the children discover for themselves what's happening on the wordless pages. Use the finger puppets while the children assist in retelling the story. The children will enjoy having their own set of puppets to create their own story. Encourage them to tell the story to their family and friends.

Find a tree to sit under and enjoy eating the apples from Grandma's basket. Invite a grandma (or two) to join you.

GRANDFATHER TANG'S STORY

by Ann Tompert, il. by Robert Andrew Parker (Crown, 1990).

Story: Grandfather Tang tells a story to Little Soo using tangrams, ancient Chinese puzzles. The fox fairies are endowed with supernatural powers and transform easily into different characters. As Grandfather tells the story, he arranges the tangrams to shape each new character.

Materials: tangrams or paper tangrams for each child, flannel board

Directions: Tell this story, rather than read it. Learn the sequence of characters as they appear in the story. Practice making the tangram characters. Make individual tangrams for each child following the directions given in the storybook. Make larger tangrams and glue flannel on the back to use on the flannel board. Provide tangram puzzle character illustrations for each child, or make a wall chart with the illustrations as a guideline for the children to follow when making their own. Encourage children to create their own characters and story.

GRANDPA'S SLIPPERS

by Joy Watson, il. by Wendy Hodder
(Ashton Scholastic, 1989).

Story: Grandpa's slippers are worn out. Grandma thinks he should have new ones, but Grandpa likes his old ones just the way they are. In an effort to get rid of them, Grandma hides them, gives them away, and throws them in the trash, but Grandpa always retrieves them. After a week, the slippers really do fall apart and Grandpa discovers that his new ones aren't so bad after all. Also available as a Big Book.

Materials: new slippers, old slippers, pattern for making slippers (see Grandparent Crafts)

Directions: To tell this story, put on a pair of old, worn-out slippers. Ask the children to repeat the refrain "Good, that's how I like them!" each time Grandpa talks back to Grandma. At the end of the story, bring out a box containing a new pair of slippers and put them on. Children will want to make their own pair of Grandpa slippers using the pattern provided.

NIGHT NOISES

by Mem Fox, il. by Terry Denton
(Harcourt Brace, 1989).

Story: Lily Laceby, a great-great-grandmother, is nearly 90. One winter evening as Lily drifts off to sleep, she dreams of the peaceful bygone days, but there are strange noises outside that arouse her dog, Butch Aggie. The noises awaken Lily to a surprise birthday party.

Materials: tea cups, teapot, tablecloth, napkins, cream, sugar, plates, cake

Directions: The children will love to participate in the reading of this great story. Ask them to read the red large print as you point out the words. They will also want to repeat the refrain "but Lily Laceby went on dreaming." As you read, make sound effects for Butch Aggie's rumbles, growls, and barks. Soon the children will be making these sounds, too. Everyone should join in to sing a robust "Happy Birthday" to Lily Laceby.

Have a tea party, with a birthday cake, if possible. Set the table with a "lace" tablecloth, cloth napkins, and pretty cups and dishes. This is a very special treat for children who are accustomed to paper and plastic tableware.

THE TROUBLE WITH GRAN

by Babette Cole (G. P. Putnam's Sons, 1987).

Story: No one suspects that Gran is an extraterrestrial being until a group of children and senior citizens go on a field trip together. Gran does her own thing at the Old Time Music Hall, at the Glamorous Grandma contest, and while playing video games.

Materials: strip of paper suitable for a mural, crayons or colored markers, alien hat (see Grandparent Crafts)

Directions: Have the children make a mural of "Gran's Alien Friends." Divide the children into groups of three or four to work on their part of the drawing. The mural can be displayed in a hallway at child height. The children will also enjoy making their very own alien hat and pretending to be aliens. Have them dramatize what they would do if they were aliens.

WHEN I GO VISITING

by Anne and Harlow Rockwell (Macmillan, 1984).

Story: A little boy visits his grandparents, who live in the city. He rides the elevator to their apartment, sleeps in the living room, and explores their seashell collection. Grandmother reads stories to him and Grandfather plays the guitar and sings.

Materials: duffle bag (as shown in story) containing teddy bear and seashell collection

Directions: Place the duffle bag or small suitcase and teddy bear beside you before reading the story. Ask the children to think about what might be inside. Open the bag to reveal its contents. Read the story and let the children discover that the bag belongs to the boy visiting his grandparents. As time permits, allow the children to tell about visits to their own grandparents' homes or encourage them to draw pictures of those homes. Some children may not have grandparents (or may not have visited them), so ask them to tell about visits to other family members or friends. Invite a grandfather to lead some singing with the children—a guitar-playing grandfather would be perfect! Use some of the songs in the Grandparent Poems and Songs section or let the guest choose the songs he wants to sing. Display the seashell collection for the children to observe.

WILLIAM AND GRANDPA

by Alice Schertle, il. by Lydia Dabcovich (Lothrop, Lee & Shepard, 1989).

Story: William visits his grandpa every summer and they enjoy the things Grandpa did when he was young. They attempt to jump on their shadows, watch the stars from the roof of the house, and drink hot chocolate. They even both know the same song.

Materials: hot chocolate with marshmallows

Directions: Read this story on a sunny day and let the children go outside to try jumping on their own shadows. Follow the recipe in Grandparent Snacks to make hot chocolate.

THE WOODEN DOLL

by Susan Bonners (Lothrop, Lee & Shepard, 1991).

Story: While Stephanie is visiting her grandparents, she longs to play with the wooden doll sitting up high on Grandma's china cabinet. When Grandfather discovers her interest in the doll, he explains the importance of the doll in their family history. Then Stephanie is surprised to discover there's a family of ten nesting dolls inside.

Materials: wooden nesting doll, nesting doll patterns (see Grandparent Crafts)

Directions: This story is rather lengthy for preschoolers, so it's best to paraphrase it. It's especially interesting to present if you have access to a wooden nesting doll (they're often available in specialty shops). Let the children play with the doll and encourage them to create their own story about it. The children will delight in making their own paper nesting dolls.

Ackerman, Karen, il. by Stephen Gammell. **SONG AND DANCE MAN** (Scholastic, 1988).

Grandpa and his grandchildren go to the attic where Grandpa puts on his tap shoes, vest, and hat and entertains the children with a song and dance he used to do in the good old days.

Ambrus, Victor. **GRANDMA, FELIX AND MUSTAPHA BISCUIT** (William Morrow, 1982).

Felix the cat, Grandma, and Long John the parrot live together happily until Grandma brings home a cute, furry hamster named Mustapha Biscuit. Some rollicking good times develop as Felix attempts to rid the house of Mustapha Biscuit.

Blos, Joan W., il. by Emily Arnold McCully. **THE GRANDPA DAYS** (Simon & Schuster, 1989).

While Philip is visiting his grandpa, he wishes they could build a rocket ship or a racing car. Grandpa explains the difference between wishes and good planning and together they agree to build a wooden sled.

Booth, Barbara D., il. by Jim LaMarche. **MANDY** (Lothrop, Lee & Shepard, 1991).

The silver pin Mandy's grandpa gave her grandma is lost somewhere in the woods. For hearing-impaired Mandy, it's risky to go out into the scary night with an impending storm to search for the prized possession, but she does. As Mandy stumbles in the dark, she finds the pin.

Bunting, Eve, il. by Donald Carrick. **THE WEDNESDAY SURPRISE** (Clarion, 1989).

Wednesday nights are special for Anna because that's when Grandma comes over with her big bag of books. Anna spends Wednesdays teaching Grandma to read. On Dad's birthday the best surprise is when Grandma reads a book to Dad.

Burningham, John. **GRANDPA** (Crown, 1984).

A little girl and her grandpa share some special moments together. They talk about worms going to heaven, staying at the beach forever, and being a captain on a long trip to Africa.

Carlstrom, Nancy White, il. by Laurel Molk. **GRANDPAPPY** (Little, Brown, 1990).

Nate visits Grandpappy's house in Maine. Together they watch a gray heron, find a four-leaf clover, and shop for supplies. Nate listens attentively as Grandpappy gives advice and tells intriguing stories.

Caseley, Judith. **GRANDPA'S GARDEN LUNCH** (Greenwillow, 1990).

Grandpa likes to work in his garden and Sarah likes to help him. Together they plant and water the seeds until they grow. Then, one day, Grandma invites Grandpa and Sarah to a special lunch made from the things that grew in their garden.

Cole, Babette. **THE TROUBLE WITH GRANDAD** (G. P. Putnam's Sons, 1988).

Grandad's enormous vegetables win all the prizes at the Vegetable Show. As a ruse, the other exhibitors give Grandad a special tomato plant that grows larger than the police station. Grandad gets into lots of trouble until he finds a solution.

Davis, Maggie S., il. by John Wallner. **GRANDMA'S SECRET LETTER** (Holiday House, 1982).

In a secret letter to her granddaughter, Grandma gives directions for getting to '

her house. Along the way, the grand-daughter is to deliver messages to the elves, the ghosts, the witches, and the dragons. Unknown to the grand-daughter, all of these creatures follow her to Grandma's house for a grand tea party.

Ehrlich, Amy, il. by Marie H. Henry. **BUNNIES AND THEIR GRANDMA** (Dial Books for Young Readers, 1985).

Three bunny children enjoy a picnic at Grandma's with their cousins. They make mischief galore as they play games and enjoy their picnic lunch. At the end of the day, the exhausted bunnies take a cozy ride home in a wheelbarrow.

Flournoy, Valerie, il. by Jerry Pinkney. **THE PATCHWORK QUILT** (Dial Books for Young Readers, 1985).

Tanya loves watching her grandmother piece her patchwork quilt using scraps of fabric belonging to various family members. When Grandmother becomes ill, Tanya finishes Grandmother's masterpiece herself.

Greenfield, Eloise, il. by Floyd Cooper. **GRANDPA'S FACE** (Philomel, 1988).

Tamika loves the way Grandfather tells stories. In fact, she and Grandpa have lots of good times together. One day, Tamika sees an angry, mean face on Grandfather when he's rehearsing for a play. She's afraid Grandpa's feelings toward her have changed, but all is resolved at the end.

Griffith, Helen V., il. by James Stevenson. **GRANDADDY'S PLACE** (Greenwillow, 1987).

Janetta and her mother travel to the country by train to visit Grandaddy's

farm. At first, Janetta doesn't like it there, but she soon becomes accustomed to the animals and discovers that they like her. She enjoys her stay and loves being with her grandaddy.

Handy, Libby, il. by James Reece. **MY POPPA LOVES OLD MOVIES** (Scholastic, 1986).

A little boy hurries home from school to tell his grandfather, Poppa, all about his day. However, Poppa is really more interested in watching an old movie on TV, and their conversation gets rather confusing.

Henriod, Lorraine, il. by Christa Chevalier. **GRANDMA'S WHEELCHAIR** (Albert Whitman, 1982).

Four-year-old Thomas spends his mornings with his grandma, who's in a wheelchair. Together they make applesauce, do the laundry, and dust furniture. Thomas even repairs the flat tire on Grandma's wheelchair.

Hines, Anna Grossnickle. **COME TO THE MEADOW** (Clarion, 1984).

Mattie's family members are too busy to go to the meadow where the spring flowers are in bloom and the clouds appear to be scoops of ice cream. However, when Mattie invites her grandma, Granny packs a picnic lunch and they go off to the meadow. The rest of Mattie's family end up joining in on the springtime fun.

Hutchins, Pat. **HAPPY BIRTHDAY, SAM** (Greenwillow Books, 1978).

It's Sam's birthday and even though he's a year older, he's still not big enough to reach the light switch or the doorknob. Then Grandfather's gift, a

little chair, arrives, and Sam's problems are solved. Sam turns the knob to open the door for Grandfather when he comes to the birthday party.

Ichikawa, Satomi. **NORA'S STARS** (Philomel, 1989).

While Nora is visiting her grandmother, the old toys in the chest come alive and bring down the stars from the sky. Nora soon discovers the sky is black and sad without its stars, so she returns them and all is well again.

Johnson, Angela, il. by David Soma. **WHEN I AM OLD WITH YOU** (Orchard, 1990).

A child imagines being old with his grandpa. They share their love for each other as they go fishing, play cards, visit the ocean, and sit in rocking chairs side by side.

Johnston, Tony, il. by Brad Sneed. **GRANDPA'S SONG** (Dial Books for Young Readers, 1991).

Grandpa's songs are so exuberant and loud they make everybody laugh, and Grandma has to hold on to the pictures hanging on the wall to keep them from falling. One day, the children notice that Grandpa has trouble remembering the songs he loves so well. They sing along with him to help him remember.

Joyce, William. **A DAY WITH WILBUR ROBINSON** (Harper & Row, 1990).

Wilbur and his best friend join the search for Grandfather Robinson's missing false teeth. In this wacky household, Uncle Judlow relaxes with his brain augmenter attached to his head, Wilbur's sister's prom dress is a skyscraper, and Cousin Laszlo flies around in his anti-gravity device. Everyone joins the search to find Grandfather's false teeth.

Keller, Holly. **THE BEST PRESENT** (Greenwillow, 1989).

Eight-year-old Rosie wants to visit her grandmother in the hospital, but she's too young. Rosie dresses up to look older, but the staff is not fooled, so Rosie sends flowers up to her grandmother with the elevator man. There isn't a card saying who the flowers are from, but Grandma knows.

Levine, Evan, il. by S. D. Schindler. **NOT THE PIANO, MRS. MEDLEY** (Orchard, 1991).

Mrs. Medley and her grandson Max set out for the beach, only to return home again and again to get more gear. Mrs. Medley insists on taking boots, games, a table, chair, an accordion, bongo drums, and so on until they have more stuff than they'll ever use, but at least she doesn't take the piano.

Levinson, Riki, il. by Diane Goode. **I GO WITH MY FAMILY TO GRANDMA'S** (E. P. Dutton, 1986).

Five cousins and their families from each of the five boroughs of New York City travel by various means of transportation to Grandma's house in Brooklyn. The family becomes livelier and livelier, but when a portrait is taken, the activity is curtailed briefly.

Lyon, George Ella, il. by Stephen Gammell. **COME A TIDE** (Orchard, 1990).

In this lighthearted account of a spring flood, Grandma says, "It'll come a tide." When the creek swells, the folks walk up the hill to Grandma's to spend the night. The next day, the weather calms down and everyone works together to dig out their treasures.

MacLachlan, Patricia, il. by Deborah Kogan Ray. **THROUGH GRANDPA'S EYES** (Harper & Row, 1980).

John sees things differently as he spends a day with his blind grandfather. Grandfather knows the sun is up when he feels the warmth, he can smell what's for breakfast, and so the day goes as they spend it together.

Martin, Bill Jr. and John Archambault, il. by Ted Rand. **KNOTS ON A COUNTING ROPE** (Holt, 1987).

In this American Indian tale, Grandfather tells Boy the story of when he was born, how he was named, and how he grew to be strong. When the story ends, Grandfather ties another knot in the rope and tells Boy that when the rope is filled with knots, he will know the story also.

McCully, Emily Arnold. **THE GRANDMA MIX-UP** (Harper & Row, 1988).

By mistake, both grandmas are invited to baby-sit when Pip's parents go on a trip. The grandmas don't agree on anything. Grandma Nan likes a neat room and wants to eat tuna with sprouts, while Grandma Sal likes to watch ball games on TV and send out for pizza. The problem is solved when it's decided to do things Pip's way.

McPhail, David. **GRANDFATHER'S CAKE** (Charles Scribner's Sons, 1979).

At their grandmother's request, two small boys and their pony set out to take a piece of cake to their grandfather, who is tending the sheep. Along the way a hungry fox, a bear, and a bandit attempt to relieve the boys of the cake. Their attempts are foiled, and, when the boys finally do reach Grandpa, they discover there are three pieces of cake in the basket.

Miller, Montzalee, il. by Katherine Potter. **MY GRANDMOTHER'S COOKIE JAR** (Price/Stern/Sloan, 1987).

Grandma passes the stories about her Indian life on to her grandchild as they enjoy eating cookies from the Indian-head cookie jar. One day, Grandfather gives the grandchild the cookie jar, which is filled with Grandma's love and stories the grandchild will pass on to her own little ones some day.

Moore, Elaine, il. by Elise Primavera. **GRANDMA'S PROMISE** (Lothrop, Lee & Shepard, 1988).

Kim has never been to Grandma's in the winter before, and she loves every minute of it. A special relationship develops as they go ice skating on the pond, feed the birds, sleep on blankets by the wood stove, and watch white-tailed deer running through the snow. GRANDMA'S HOUSE is another enjoyable story about Kim and her grandma.

Root, Phyllis and Carol A. Marron, il. by Deborah Kogan Ray. **GRETCHEN'S GRANDMA** (Raintree, 1983).

Gretchen's grandmother came from Germany for a visit. The only German word Gretchen knows is "Ona," which means grandma. The two of them don't know each other's language, but they are able to communicate and share their love.

Scott, Ann Herbert, il. by Meg Kelleher Aubrey. **GRANDMOTHER'S CHAIR** (Clarion, 1990).

Four-year-old Katie wonders how her grandmother ever fit into the little black-and-gold chair. Katie and Grandmother

look through the photo album together and discover all the little girls—Katie's great-grandmother, grandmother, and mother—sitting in the chair. Now the chair belongs to Katie, and some day she will give it to her little girl.

Shecter, Ben. **GRANDMA REMEMBERS** (Harper & Row, 1989).

A boy and his grandmother take a final look through the house where his grandparents lived. They relive memories of the many wonderful times they shared there. They lock the door and Grandmother is ready for new adventures in a new home. The boy promises to always be there when she becomes lonely.

Silverman, Erica, il. by Deborah Kogan Ray. **ON GRANDMA'S ROOF** (Macmillan, 1990).

Emily's favorite day is laundry day at Grandma's. They carry the wet clothes to the roof, where the clothes are hung up to dry. They play and dance around the clothes and laugh together. They spread a blanket and enjoy a picnic lunch. The glorious day ends when the clothes are dry and taken down.

Stevenson, James. **COULD BE WORSE** (Mulberry, 1977).

Everything is always the same at Grandpa's house until one morning when he relates the adventures he had the night before. A large bird pulled him out of bed, dropped him on a mountain, and then he flew home on a paper airplane.

Tarlton, John. **GOING TO GRANDMA'S** (Scholastic, 1987).

A little girl gives 12 reasons why she dislikes going to Grandma's. She doesn't

like to take a bath and dress up. She doesn't like loading the car and stopping for gas, and so on. There is only one reason why she likes going to Grandma's. She loves being there. Also available as a Big Book.

Waddell, Martin, il. by Dom Mansell. **MY GREAT GRANDPA** (G. P. Putnam's Sons, 1990).

A little girl and her great-grandpa have a very special relationship. Great-Grandpa might be weak and his legs might not move well, but he knows things that no one else knows, and he shares these thoughts with his little granddaughter as they go on a walk together.

Ward, Sally G. **PUNKY SPENDS THE DAY** (E. P. Dutton, 1989).

A little girl named Punky spends a happy day with Gram and Grampy. Punky builds a hideout with blankets, hides in the raked leaves, and then gets ready for a bedtime story. But Gram and Grampy are asleep by the time she's ready.

Williams, Barbara, il. by Kay Chorao. **KEVIN'S GRANDMA** (E. P. Dutton, 1975).

When Kevin's grandma comes to visit, she rides on a motorcycle and brings Mad magazine and peanut-butter soup. She gives judo lessons, scuba dives, drinks tiger's milk, and does many other wild and fantastic things that Kevin loves.

Ziefert, Harriet, il. by Deborah Kogan Ray. **WITH LOVE FROM GRANDMA** (Viking Kestrel, 1989).

Grandma wants to knit something special for her young granddaughter Sarah. Sarah chooses her favorite colors of yarn and watches and waits anxiously as Grandma knits the afghan. It is completed just in time to keep her warm on cold winter days.

Grandparent Poems and Songs

MY GRANDMOTHER

My grandmother is very old,
Her clock has lost its chime.
She wants to wind it up again,
But, she can't find the time.

LITTLE GIRL, LITTLE GIRL

Little girl, little girl,
Where have you been?
I've been to see grandmother
Over the green.
What did she give you?
Milk in a can.
What did you say for it?
Thank you, Grandam.
—Mother Goose

More Grandparent Poems

"Grandfather Gander," p. 26 and
"Grandma Bear," p. 36, in RIDE A PURPLE
PELICAN by Jack Prelutsky, il. by Garth
Williams (Greenwillow, 1986).

"Growing Old, Grandpapa" and
"Grandpa Dropped His Glasses," p. 159,
and "The Shark," p. 177, in THE RANDOM
HOUSE BOOK OF POETRY FOR CHILDREN,
selected by Jack Prelutsky, il. by Marc
Brown (Random House, 1983).

"Ruthless Rhyme," p. 14 and
"Grandpapa," p. 30, in FOR LAUGHING
OUT LOUD: POEMS TO TICKLE YOUR
FUNNYBONE, selected by Jack Prelutsky,
il. by Marjorie Priceman (Knopf, 1991).

WHERE IS GRANDPA?
(Tune: "Are You Sleeping")

Where is Grandpa,
Where is Grandpa? (Shrug shoulders.)
I miss him, I miss him. (Make sad face.)
How I wish he'd visit,
How I wish he'd visit, (Motion toward
    self.)
I love him, I love him. (Hug self.)

I'M GOING TO GRANDMA'S
(Tune: "I'm a Little Teapot")

I'm going to Grandma's,
Yes, I am.
We are going to eat
Some scones and jam.
Then we'll take a short walk
Down the lane.
At dinner time we'll
Stroll back home again.

CAN YOUR GRANDMA BAKE?
(Tune: "Do Your Ears Hang Low?")

Can your grandma bake
Frosted-covered chocolate cake
Or a wiggling Jell-O mold
That you, giggling, try to hold.
Can she make some nice spaghetti
(Don't you want dinner already?)
Can your grandma bake?

Repeat for Grandpa.

More Grandparent Songs

"Over the River and Through the
Woods," p. 57, in WEE SING by Pamela
Conn Beall and Susan Hagen Nipp
(Price/Stern/ Sloan, 1985).

WHO AM I?

(This game only works with children who can read.)

Prepare a piece of paper for each child. On each piece write the name of a storybook character who appears in a story the children have read; for example, Grandfather Tang, Gran, Sarah, Punky, or Kevin's grandma. Pin a name on the back of each child and explain that the object of the game is to guess which character is pinned to his or her back. Each child asks other children questions about the person whose name is pinned on his or her back, such as, "Am I a boy?" "Am I a grandparent?" "Do I live in the city?" Only "Yes" or "No" questions are permitted. As soon as a child thinks he or she knows the pinned-on name, he or she can go to the director of the game and make a guess. If the guess is correct, the player spends the rest of the time answering other children's questions. If the guess is incorrect, the player continues to play.

GRANDMOTHER'S MEMORY WORD GAME

Before playing this game, read the following book to the children: I UNPACKED MY GRANDMOTHER'S TRUNK by Susan Ramsay Hoguet (E. P. Dutton, 1983).

In this game, the first player says, "I unpacked my grandmother's trunk and I took out an airplane" (or any object beginning with the letter a). The second player repeats the line and adds an object beginning with the letter "b." The game continues until all 26 letters are used. The last person will try to repeat all 26 words in alphabetical order. Adjust the game to the ability of the players (for example, objects would not have to be in alphabetical order).

GRANDPA AND GRANDMA DRAMATIZATION

Provide "grandparent" play clothes in the dress-up center to encourage grandparent dramatizations. Include items such as high heels, fancy hats, dresses, aprons, suit jackets, vests, ties, and men's shoes. Encourage the children to create a grandparent-theme play that can be presented to the class or other classes.

DRAMATIZE COCO CAN'T WAIT

Use the Grandma and Coco finger puppets (see Grandparent Crafts) to dramatize this story. Two people do the dramatization, each with a puppet, or one person can use both puppets, one on each hand. Have the children reenact the sequence of events as Coco and Grandma travel back and forth between the houses, missing each other but finally meeting in the middle. Then let them enjoy eating the goodies in Grandma's basket.

NESTING DOLLS

Materials: doll patterns, markers or crayons, scissors, stapler, glue (optional), poster paper (optional)

Directions: Copy all five doll patterns for each child. Have them color and cut out the dolls. Then have them fasten the tabs in a circle and staple together. If desired, they can glue the largest doll onto a piece of poster paper to hold all the dolls together as one is placed inside the other.

GRANDFATHER TANG'S TANGRAM

Materials: tangram pattern, colored poster paper, scissors, carbon paper

Directions: Use carbon paper to transfer the tangram pattern onto colored poster paper and cut out to make individual tangrams. See GRANDFATHER TANG'S STORY in the Read-Aloud section for suggestions for use.

GRANDPA'S SLIPPERS

Materials: slipper pattern, scissors, colored tagboard, stapler

Directions: After reading GRANDPA'S SLIPPERS, use this pattern as a guideline for the children to cut out and make their own slippers. Staple the slipper toe around the slipper sole. Don't forget to have the children make a left and a right. They'll think it's fun to pretend they're Grandpa while wearing the slippers. Encourage the children to dramatize the story or create their own story using the slippers as props.

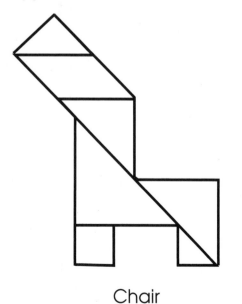

Chair

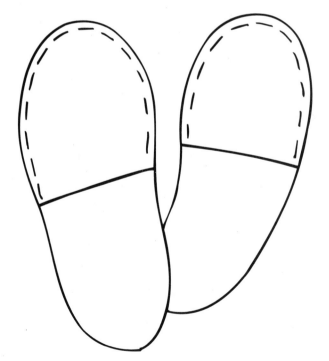

FINGER PUPPETS

Materials: puppet patterns, white tagboard, scissors, markers or crayons

Directions: Copy the patterns below onto tagboard and let the children color and add features to them using the patterns as a guideline. Help the children cut out the puppets and the holes for fingers. Have them insert their fingers in the holes to dramatize how Grandmother and Coco kept missing each other. Use this activity after reading COCO CAN'T WAIT.

GRAN'S ALIEN HAT

Materials: colored crepe paper, bright colored or sparkly pipe cleaners, lightweight tagboard or construction paper, stapler, glue, small buttons, macaroni or sequins, scissors

Directions: For each hat band, cut a piece of tagboard 1 1/2" by 24" and staple together to fit each child's head. Cut a 12" diameter circle from the crepe paper. (It's easier if you use a plate or lid as a pattern.) Tuck the edges of the circle into the band, and glue or staple in place. Let the children insert as many pipe cleaners as desired into the band and staple in place. They can glue buttons onto the ends of the pipe cleaners, and decorate the band with sequins or macaroni.

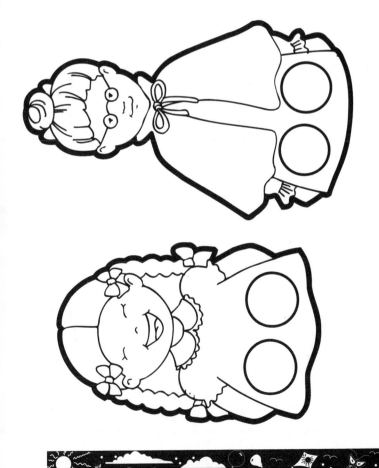

Slipper Patterns

Tangram Pattern

chair

No. 7

boat

candle

No. 2

horse and rider

Don't forget to create your own designs!

Doll Patterns

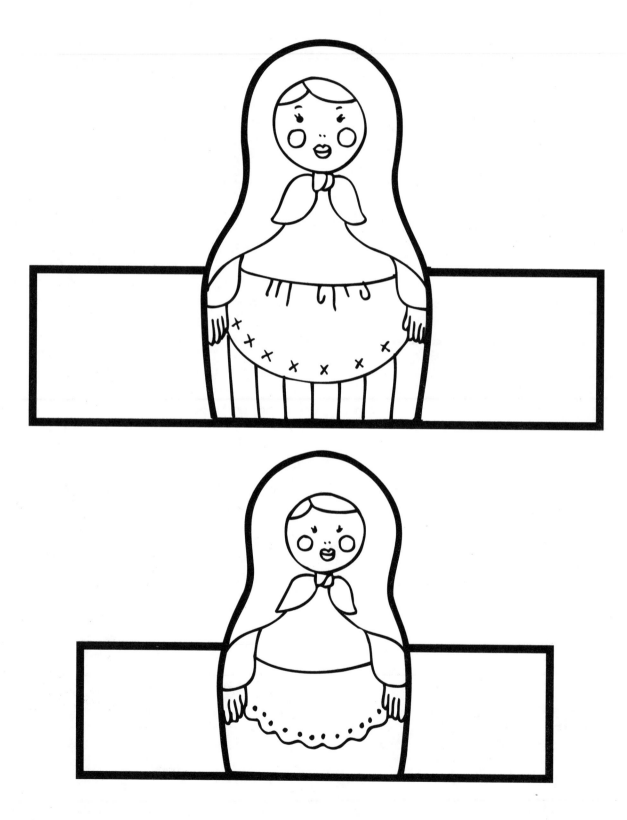

Doll Patterns

GRANDFATHER'S CAKE

Make your favorite chocolate cake mix, cut the cake into pieces, and put the pieces into a basket just like Grandma's in the story GRANDFATHER'S CAKE by David McPhail. After reading the story, the children will be pleasantly surprised to see the basket filled with cake. Perhaps you'll want to invite a grandfather to share the cake with the children.

HOT CHOCOLATE WITH MARSHMALLOWS

milk
miniature marshmallows
chocolate syrup

1. Heat the desired amount of milk on the stove until hot, being careful not to scorch. (Adults should do this part.)

2. Give each child a cup of hot milk, a spoon, and a few miniature marsh-mallows.

3. Pass a bottle of chocolate syrup around for each child to add to the hot milk. Have them stir the mixture and add the marshmallows. Remind the children that the drink is hot, and that they should sip it slowly. This treat is especially appropriate after reading WILLIAM AND GRANDPA by Alice Shertle.

GRANDMA'S PORRIDGE

After reading GRANDMA'S SECRET LETTER by Maggie Davis (or other stories that include porridge), the children will enjoy tasting some porridge.

1 cup rolled oats (not instant)
2 1/2 cups milk
honey (optional)
dried or fresh fruit

Combine the oats and milk in a saucepan and bring to a boil. Stir occasionally. Simmer for 10 to 15 minutes until soft. Add more milk if necessary. Serve with honey if desired. Top with the children's favorite dried or fresh fruit. Serves 4.

A good classroom should be a home to many books, and many of these books will be about characters who live in a wide variety of homes: trailers, motor homes, apartments, houseboats, tents, log cabins, condominiums, and houses made of straw, twigs, and bricks (just ask the three little pigs!).

Children will soon learn that something as simple as an umbrella or a blanket over a table can be a home for playing or reading. They'll also find that tree houses are a world of fun, and great places to read a book. But though they may learn about many different people's and characters' homes, they'll probably feel that, although other houses are fun to visit, their own home is the very best place of all.

SETTING THE STAGE

Encourage the children to bring to school some type of home to use in a display: an abandoned bird nest, an empty snail shell or seashell, or any object that serves as a house in a storybook (the mouse in IF YOU GIVE A MOUSE A COOKIE takes a nap in a face-powder box). Next to the display, erect a sign saying "Home Sweet Home." Refer to A HOUSE IS A HOUSE FOR ME by Mary Ann Hoberman for additional ideas.

In the reading center, use a large doll house to store books. Arrange a blanket over the reading center to make a roof. Put up a tepee to use for reading only. Ready-made tepees are available in toy stores or through toy catalogs. Write to the following address for a tepee pattern: Klaus B. Rau Company, P. O. Box 1236, Coeur d'Alene, ID 83814. Or write to Troll Learn & Play, 100 Corporate Drive, Mahwah, NJ 07430 for a catalog to purchase a ready-made tepee.

Build a cardboard castle using the illustration provided in this chapter as a guideline. Cut one large sheet of cardboard for the front. Cover with brick-designed contact paper or spray-paint grey and draw on lines to simulate bricks or stones. Cut two side pieces and attach with masking tape to the front. This will allow the castle to be free-standing. Provide a few props, such as prince and princess clothes and shining (plastic) armor for make-believe play. Also make sure to display books about castles, dragons, and kings and queens.

BULLETIN BOARD IDEAS

1. Enlarge and copy the "A Houseful of Books" illustration. Color and cut out. Cut out all but one side of the windows and door so they will open and close as if hinged. Behind the windows and door adhere titles of books that will be read aloud. Display at an appropriate height to permit children to open and close the windows and door. Let the children choose each day's story by opening a window or door.

2. Cut out and color copies of the characters from THE NAPPING HOUSE by Audrey Wood and make a flannel board by attaching a piece of flannel to the back of each picture. Make a flannel-backed paper bed, and place the characters on the flannel board in the proper order as they arrive to sleep on the bed. The children will enjoy retelling the story as they manipulate the flannel board pieces themselves.

A HOUSEFUL OF BOOKS

Castle Pattern

THE BIG ORANGE SPLOT

by Daniel Manus Pinkwater (Scholastic, 1977).

Story: A bird drops orange paint on Mr. Plumbean's house, leaving an orange splot on the roof. Mr. Plumbean leaves the splot and paints the rest of his house in a psychedelic pattern. Eventually, his neighbors decide that they like his house and paint their own homes in very unusual ways.

Materials: paper, colored markers, paints or crayons

Directions: Don't show the illustrations when reading this story; let the children draw pictures of what they imagine the houses look like. Later, show the children the author's perception of the house. Refer to Home Crafts, Home Songs, and Home Snacks for ideas related to this story.

THE BIGGEST HOUSE IN THE WORLD

by Leo Lionni (Pantheon, 1968).

Story: Several snails live happily on a cabbage plant. One snail expresses his desire to have the biggest house in the world. After the snail's father tells it the story about a snail whose house was so big it couldn't move, the little snail decides it's best to keep his house small.

Materials: snail or snail shells

Directions: Bring various kinds of snail shells for the children to observe before reading this story. After hearing the story, let the children draw and color their own version of the snail's big house.

IS THIS A HOUSE FOR HERMIT CRAB?
by Megan McDonald, il. by S. D. Schindler (Orchard, 1990).

Story: Hermit Crab outgrows his old home and ventures into the world to find a new one. He goes scritch-scratch across the ocean sand. He finds several homes, but they don't fit properly. When the pricklepine fish comes to eat Hermit Crab, he finds a snail shell for his new safe home.

Materials: crab puppet (see Resources for ordering Folkmanis puppets), rock, tin can, driftwood, plastic pail, container of sand, fishing net, snail shell

Directions: While reading the story, ask the children to join in on the "scritch, scratch" phrases. Retell the story using a crab puppet and the items listed above. Let the children help you by holding up the various props as they appear in the story. Leave the props in the room to encourage the children to retell the story on their own.

LOUISE BUILDS A HOUSE
by Louise Pfanner (Orchard, 1987).

Story: Louise builds her dream house in her imagination. It begins with a flat roof (for flying kites) and becomes more and more elaborate as she adds gardens, bees, trees, a clock, a moat, and a boat.

Materials: drawing paper, markers or paint

Directions: After reading the story, the children will want to draw their own dream house. Encourage them to use lots of imagination. Or have the children cooperate drawing one large house, with each child making his or her own contribution. One child might draw the frame of the house, another the trees, and so on.

MOUSEKIN'S GOLDEN HOUSE

by Edna Miller (Prentice-Hall, 1964).

Story: Mousekin discovers a rejected jack-o'-lantern near his forest home. He ventures inside the pumpkin and decides to move in. When winter comes, the pumpkin closes its eyes, nose, and mouth to make Mousekin's home warm and comfy.

Materials: stuffed toy mouse, jack-o'-lantern, scraps of paper, construction paper, markers

Directions: Before reading the story, introduce Mousekin, the stuffed mouse, to the children. Explain that the mouse lives in a chestnut log in the forest until one day he finds a new home. After hearing the story, the children will enjoy making Mousekin's golden house out of paper and markers. To illustrate the story, scraps of paper can be placed inside the jack-o'-lantern to make a cozy bed for the toy mouse.

OSCAR MOUSE FINDS A HOME

by Moira Miller, il. by Maria Majewska (Dial, 1985).

Story: Oscar Mouse lives in a crowded, noisy attic with all his little brothers and sisters, who pester him constantly. In his search for a new home, Oscar finds an owl's nest, a soft bed with a loud snorer, and a powder puff. None of these is satisfactory, but soon Oscar finds an empty sugar can that becomes his "Home Sweet Home."

Materials: mouse puppet or stuffed toy mouse, can with lid, "Home Sweet Home" sign, paper scraps

Directions: Hold up the "Home Sweet Home" sign. Discuss with the children the meaning of the sign. Read the story, showing the illustrations. Hold up the can. Put some torn pieces of paper and the stuffed mouse in it. Make the filled can available for the children to play with later. Modify the sign to read "Oscar's Home Sweet Home."

PERCY AND THE FIVE HOUSES

by Else Holmelund Minarik, il. by James Stevenson (Greenwillow, 1989).

Story: Percy is a very fortunate beaver because Ferd the fox has made him a member of "The House of the Month Club." Percy will receive a new house every month. First, he receives a cardboard house, then a castle, a tepee, a motor camper, and an igloo—none of which is satisfactory. He decides to slide into the water, which is the best home of all for a beaver.

Materials: copies of the "House of the Month Club" membership cards (see below), igloo and tepee (see Home Crafts), castle (see beginning of chapter)

Directions: Make enough copies of the "House of the Month Club" membership card for each child to have one. Discuss the benefits of owning such a card. After reading the story, the children will want to make some of Percy's houses as described in the story. Divide the class into groups of three or four to make the houses. They can take turns playing with a different house for a designated amount of time.

THIS IS THE PLACE FOR ME

by Joanna Cole, il. by William Van Horn (Scholastic, 1986).

Story: Morty the bear is too big for his house, so he decides to find a new one. His hilarious adventures take him to several different houses but, ironically, his own house is really the best place for him after all.

Materials: toy bear dressed as Morty, brown paper, markers, tape, toy dragon

Directions: Ask the children to repeat with you the phrase "This is the place for me" as the story is read. Make a small tepee to put on the toy bear's head, and curl him up with the stuffed dragon. Make the stuffed toys available for the children to play with. Or make flannel board patterns for all of the characters. Encourage the children to use these props to recreate the story.

is a member of the
House of the Month Club.

Ferd the Fox

Aardema, Verna, il. by Leo and Diane Dillon. **WHO'S IN RABBIT'S HOUSE?** (Dial, 1977).

In this Masai folk tale, Rabbit can't get into her house because The Long One is hiding inside. It threatens to trample the jackal, the leopard, the elephant, and the rhinoceros if Rabbit attempts to harm it. Finally, the frog pretends to be a cobra to get The Long One to leave. When it does, the animals discover that The Long One is really a caterpillar.

Andersen, Hans Christian, adapted by Anthea Bell, il. by Jean Claverie. **THE OLD HOUSE** (North-South Books, 1984).

A bright-eyed little boy befriends a lonely old man who lives in a very old magical house across a busy city street. The boy sends the man a gift of a tin soldier, which reappears many years later when the boy is grown and comes back to visit the spot where the house used to be.

Bauer, Caroline Feller, il. by Diane Paterson. **TOO MANY BOOKS** (Viking, 1986).

Maralou loves books so much that she receives them for birthdays, holidays, and for just about any reason. Soon her house is so full of books there's no place to sit or walk or even get out the door.

Biro, Val. **THE WIND IN THE WILLOWS: HOME SWEET HOME** (Simon & Schuster, 1987).

At the first snowfall, Mole and Walter Rat return to Mole's home, which he had abandoned. The home is cold and dusty, but Walter Rat soon helps make it a warm, comfortable home, and sad Mole becomes happy again.

Bodden, Ilona, il. by Hans Poppel. **WHEN THE MOON SHINES BRIGHTLY ON THE HOUSE** (Houghton Mifflin, 1991).

At night when the house is quiet and everyone is asleep, the moon shines overhead and a mouse comes out of his hole. The moonlight glimmers and lights the mouse's way as he goes from room to room having fun.

Bunting, Eve, il. by Ronald Himler. **FLY AWAY HOME** (Clarion, 1991).

A small boy and his father live in a large airport. They comfort each other as they avoid security guards, make good friends, and share their hope for the future when they might have a home of their own.

Burton, Virginia Lee. **THE LITTLE HOUSE** (Houghton Mifflin, 1969).

A little house is built on a hill in the country. It loves being there, but as the years pass, the country grows into a city and the little house becomes surrounded by skyscrapers and noisy trains and cars. Luckily, a smart lady rescues the little house and returns it to the countryside.

Carle, Eric. **A HOUSE FOR HERMIT CRAB** (Picture Book Studio, 1987).

Hermit Crab keeps outgrowing his shell houses! When he does find a shell big enough, it's quite bare, so he decorates it to protect it from sea anemones, coral, sea urchins, and lantern fish.

Cole, Joanna and Philip, il. by William Van Horn. **HANK AND FRANK FIX UP THE HOUSE** (Scholastic, 1988).

Hank and Frank fix up houses just like new. By mistake they fix up Mr. Grumble's house with some drastic changes:

a big fish pond in the floor, a real tiger for a rug, and big palm trees throughout the house. Mr. Grumble is quite upset at first, but eventually he gets used to his new home.

Demarest, Chris L. **BENEDICT FINDS A HOME** (Lothrop, Lee & Shepard, 1982).

Benedict, a bright bluebird, lives in a crowded, noisy nest with his many brothers and sisters. One day, he decides to search for his own home. Benedict tries out a tree, a shoe, a shiny horn, and a statue, but discovers his old home is best.

De Regniers, Beatrice Schenk, il. by Irene Haas. **A LITTLE HOUSE OF YOUR OWN** (Harcourt Brace, 1954).

Everybody should have a special, private house, whether it's a cardboard box or space under the dining room table. Any place can be a house where one can enjoy peace and quiet . . . as long as other people respect it.

Dragonwagon, Crescent, il. by Jerry Pinkney. **HOME PLACE** (Macmillan, 1990).

While on a hike, a family finds some blooming daffodils, a piece of a china plate, a doll's arm, and a half chimney. The clues reveal that they've stumbled on the site of an old house. The family then imagines who lived in the house and how they might have spent their lives.

Dupasquier, Philippe. **OUR HOUSE ON THE HILL** (Viking Kestral, 1988).

This wordless book depicts month by month how the house on the hill changes through the seasons. Snowball fights in January, summer fun in July, and getting ready for Christmas in December.

Eversole, Robyn Harbert, il. by Peter Palagonia. **THE MAGIC HOUSE** (Orchard, 1992).

April believes her house at 519 Kipperney Street is magical. There's a waterfall down the stairs, and the living room is a desert. April's older sister, Meredith, doesn't believe her until Meredith turns into a beautiful swan while dancing on the blue lake in the front hall.

Gackenbach, Dick. **ALICE'S SPECIAL ROOM** (Clarion, 1991).

Alice tells her mother that she has a special room where she can lie on the beach in January and ride a sled in July. Mother looks all through the house before realizing that the special room is in Alice's imagination.

Hayward, Linda, il. by Lynn Munsinger. **HELLO HOUSE** (Random House, 1988).

Brer Wolf attempts to trick Brer Rabbit's family by hiding in their house. However, Brer Rabbit suspects something is amiss, and talks to the house to trick Brer Wolf into answering. Brer Wolf leaves the house as a very defeated wolf.

Hoberman, Mary Ann, il. by Betty Fraser. **A HOUSE IS A HOUSE FOR ME** (Penguin Books, 1987).

In rhyme, this book depicts a profusion of houses for various animals and objects. A coop is for chickens, a glove for a hand, a hill for an ant, and a pot for potatoes. Also available as a Big Book.

THE HOUSE THAT JACK BUILT: A Mother Goose Nursery Rhyme (Holiday House, 1985), il. by Janet Stevens.

This popular cumulative rhyme relates a chain of events beginning with the malt that lay in the house that Jack built.

Krauss, Ruth, il. by Maurice Sendak. **A VERY SPECIAL HOUSE** (Harper & Row, 1953).

In this Caldecott Honor Book, a little boy describes his very special house. This silly house can do anything because it is imaginary.

LeSieg, Theo., il. by Richard Erdoes. **COME OVER TO MY HOUSE** (Random House, 1966).

In rhyme, many different types of houses are described in a delightful way. Some houses are pink, some are tall, and some are small, but whatever kind of house it might be, the reader is always invited to come over.

LeSieg, Theo., il. by Roy McKie. **IN A PEOPLE HOUSE** (Random House, 1972).

Mouse invites Mr. Bird inside to show him what's in a People House. There are things like roller skates, stairs, bananas, doughnuts, a hammer, and people who shoo them out the door.

Mahy, Margaret, il. by Wendy Smith. **KEEPING HOUSE** (McElderry, 1991).

Lizzie Firkin works every night singing and dancing in a famous club. She's so busy she doesn't have time to clean her house, and it becomes very untidy. The cat sleeps in the bread box and hair-dye bottles clutter the piano. Lizzie finally hires a housekeeper, but cleans the house herself before he arrives.

Maris, Ron. **IS ANYONE HOME?** (Greenwillow, 1985).

A young child visits his grandparents' farm and discovers who lives in each home. The chickens have their own home and so do the cats, dogs, and horses. A flap in the book serves as a door each time a new home is found.

Mayne, William, il. by Sarah Fox-Davis. **A HOUSE IN TOWN** (Prentice-Hall, 1987).

A family of foxes lives in the cellar of a house in town until the house is torn down. In their search for a new home, the fox family is bothered by a pack of dogs. However, the family escapes when the drawbridge is raised and the dogs can no longer follow them.

Miller, Moira and Maria Majewska. **OSCAR MOUSE FINDS A HOME** (Scholastic, 1989).

Oscar explores the house in an attempt to find a spot to claim as his own. He tries crawling under a powder puff and joining a collection of stuffed animals. Finally, he finds a forgotten corner of the house and he spruces it up with shredded newspaper.

Novak, Matt. **ELMER BLUNT'S OPEN HOUSE** (Orchard, 1992).

When Elmer leaves his door ajar as he hurries off to work, several woodland animals enter and make themselves at home. The animals even frighten away a prospective burglar. When Elmer comes home, the animals hide beneath his bed and escape after he falls asleep.

Peppe, Rodney. **THE MICE WHO LIVED IN A SHOE** (Lothrop, Lee & Shepard, 1981).

Life is not good for a family of mice who live in an old shoe. They have no protection from nasty weather or the neighborhood cat. Everyone works together to build a dream house in the shoe, and they all live happily ever after.

Rice, Eve, il. by Nancy Winslow Parker. **GRAMMY'S HOUSE** (Greenwillow, 1990).

Grammy's house is a very special place to her grandchildren, who come to visit

every Sunday. The house smells of delicious things to eat. The children milk the cow and make butter. At the end of the day, Grammy sends home pieces of chocolate cake with the grandchildren, and says goodbye until next Sunday.

Rockwell, Anne. **IN OUR HOUSE** (Crowell, 1985).

Bear's house is warm and cozy, and each room has a variety of wonderful things. The family watches TV in the living room, packs their lunches in the kitchen, and plays Ping-Pong in the basement. All these activities make their house a home.

Schertle, Alice, il. by Meredith Dunham. **IN MY TREEHOUSE** (Lothrop, Lee & Shepard, 1983).

A child loves being in his tree house where he enjoys his solitude and independence. He spends a night there and has lots of good books to read. Best of all, he has time for lots of imaginary adventures.

Shapp, Martha and Charles, il. by Tomie de Paola. **LET'S FIND OUT ABOUT HOUSES** (Franklin Watts, 1975).

People live in houses, but not all houses are the same. There are tents, trailer houses, houseboats, and houses on stilts. Houses are made of mud, wood, bricks, grass, and ice. Houses may be very different, but they all make comfortable and happy homes.

Slate, Joseph, il. by Ashley Wolff. **WHO IS COMING TO OUR HOUSE?** (G. P. Putnam's Sons, 1988).

Mouse says someone is coming to the house. All the animals bustle around to clean up the stable. When nighttime arrives, everything is ready for the

visitors. Then the animals learn that Mary and Joseph are coming to their house for the first Christmas.

Van Laan, Nancy, il. by Marjorie Priceman. **A MOUSE IN MY HOUSE** (Knopf, 1990).

A young boy imagines his house contains a playful ape, an angry bug, a small mouse, and other creatures who all get into lots of mischief. The boy believes the rambunctious animals act just like him.

Wheeler, Cindy, il. by Stella Ormai. **A NEW HOUSE FOR LITTLE MOUSE** (Happy House Books, 1987).

When Little Mouse's old house is in need of repair, he decides to find a new one to move into. He tries the homes of his friends Little Bird, Baby Bunny, and Big Bear, but none of these is satisfactory. He goes back home to fix up his old house and then decides the nicest kind of house is your own.

Wood, Audrey, il. by Don Wood. **THE NAPPING HOUSE** (Scholastic, 1987).

This cumulative rhyme begins with Granny snoring on the bed. A dreaming child climbs on top of Granny, then a dozing dog, and so on. At the end, they all fall out of bed.

Zelinsky, Paul O. **THE MAID AND THE MOUSE AND THE ODD-SHAPED HOUSE** (Dodd & Mead, 1981).

This is a "Tell and Draw Story" in which a wee maid and a fat white mouse live happily in their odd-shaped house. As they make improvements to the house, it turns into a cat and they run away to live in an ordinary house.

THERE WAS A CROOKED MAN

There was a crooked man,
Who walked a crooked mile.
He found a crooked sixpence
Against a crooked stile.
He bought a crooked cat,
Which caught a crooked mouse,
And they all lived together
In a little crooked house.
—Mother Goose

THERE WAS A LITTLE GREEN HOUSE

There was a little green house,
And in the little green house
There was a little brown house,
And in the little brown house
There was a little yellow house,
And in the little yellow house
There was a little white house,
And in the little white house
There was a little mouse.
—Mother Goose

THE VERY NICEST PLACE

The fish live in the brook,
The birds live in the tree,
But home's the very nicest place
For a little child like me.
—Anonymous

LITTLE TOMMY TITTLEMOUSE

Little Tommy Tittlemouse
Lived in a little house.
He caught fishes
In other men's ditches.
Little Tommy Tittlemouse
Lived in a bell house.
The bell house broke,
Tommy Tittlemouse awoke.
—Mother Goose

More Home Poems

"Tree House," p. 99 and "Houses," p. 101, in SING A SONG OF POPCORN selected by Beatrice Schenk de Regniers et al. (Scholastic, 1988).

"Enter This Deserted House," p. 56, in WHERE THE SIDEWALK ENDS by Shel Silverstein (Harper & Row, 1974).

OLD MR. PLUMBEAN HAD A HOUSE

(Tune: "Old MacDonald Had a Farm")

Old Mr. Plumbean has a house,
E-I-E-I-O!
And on his house he has a splot,
E-I-E-I-O!
With a splot, splot here,
And a splot, splot there,
Here a splot, there a splot,
Everywhere a splot, splot.
Old Mr. Plumbean has a house,
E-I-E-I-O!

Old Mr. Plumbean has a house,
E-I-E-I-O!
And in his house he has a jungle,
E-I-E-I-O!
With an elephant here and an elephant there,
Here an elephant, there an elephant,
Everywhere an elephant.
Old Mr. Plumbean has a house,
E-I-E-I-O!

Old Mr. Plumbean has a house,
E-I-E-I-O!
And in his house he has a clock,
E-I-E-I-O!
With a tick-tock here,
And a tick-tock there,
Here a tick, there a tock,
Everywhere a tick-tock.
Old Mr. Plumbean has a house,
E-I-E-I-O!

The children will want to continue creating their own verses. Sing in conjunction with the reading of THE BIG ORANGE SPLOT.

More Home Songs

"Little Cabin in the Woods," p. 27 and "Over the River," p. 57, in WEE SING by Pamela Conn Beall and Susan Hagen Nipp (Price/Stern/Sloan, 1982).

"Yellow Submarine," p. 74 and "Little Brown Jug," p. 66, in THE READER'S DIGEST CHILDREN'S SONG BOOK (Reader's Digest General Books, 1985).

"Home Sweet Home" by Henry Bishop, and "The Old Folks at Home" and "My Old Kentucky Home" by Stephen Foster.

MY HOUSE HAS TWO WINDOWS

My house has two windows (Point to eyes.)
That are shiny and bright.
I close the two curtains (Shut eyes.)
To shut out the light.
It's fun to open and shut. (Open and close eyes.)
First it's dark, then it's light.
I see your two windows. (Point to someone.)
Is it daytime or night?

MANY HOUSES

Here's a nest for a blue jay. (Cup hands.)
Here's an igloo for an Eskimo. (Fit cupped hands together.)
Here's a hole for a rabbit.
(Fit thumbs and index fingers together to form circle.)
And here's a home for me, just so!
(Place arms above head in V-shape to form roof.)

ROUND AND ROUND THE VILLAGE
(Tune: "Go In and Out the Windows")

Go round and round the village,
Go round and round the village,
Go round and round the village,
As we have done before.

(Form circle holding hands. One child
skips around the outside of the circle
while everyone sings.)

Go in and out the windows,
Go in and out the windows,
Go in and out the windows,
As we have done before.

(The players raise their arms to form
windows. The child who skipped around
the circle picks a partner to go through
the windows with. Repeat the verses,
adding a child each time until there's
no one left in the circle.)

A MONSTER IN THE HOUSE

A monster in the house!
Run for your life!
Where is the husband?
Where is his wife?
They went to visit Grandma,
Who lives in Spokane.
The monster will devour the children,
If they don't come home by ten.

The children hold hands and continue to
move around in a circle while one
player—the monster—runs around inside
the circle scaring them. The husband
and wife hold hands and walk around
the outside of the circle. On the last line,
all stop, count to ten, and then the

husband and wife enter the circle to
frighten away the monster. Have
children take turns being the monster,
the husband, and the wife.

WE'RE GOING HOME

Now we're going home,
Now we're going home.
It is, it is a long way home.
Now we're going home,
Now we're going home.
It is, it is a long way home.
—Danish Folk Song

As they say this chant, have the children
form a double circle, with one circle
inside the other and the two moving in
opposite directions. Or have the
children walk in two or more lines. Have
the children do this activity when it's
time to go home for the day.

CARDBOARD HOUSE

Materials: large cardboard cartons, markers or paint, scissors or knife

Directions: Check at furniture and appliance stores for large cartons. Mark and cut out windows and a door. Provide markers or paint for the children to decorate the cartons with whatever designs they like. This is a great follow-up activity to reading THE BIG ORANGE SPLOT.

STAND-UP HOUSE

Materials: stand-up house pattern, paper, scissors, markers or crayons

Directions: Copy a house pattern for each child. Cut out and fold to stand up. Let the children color and design their houses. Help them cut along three sides of the windows and door so they can open (as if hinged). Encourage the children to draw furniture, people, curtains, etc., that can be seen when the windows and door are open. Stand finished houses on a shelf or table to create a neighborhood street. You can also enlarge the house pattern and use it as a prop when telling HELLO HOUSE by Linda Hayward. The pattern could also be used as an invitation or a greeting card.

THE BIG ORANGE SPLOT HOUSE

Materials: house pattern, colored markers or crayons, scissors, colored paper, tape

Directions: Make copies of the house pattern and encourage the children to color and design a house they would like to live in on Mr. Plumbean's street. On a long wall, tape sheets of blue, green, and grey paper to represent the sky, grass, and street. Also tape up a "Mr. Plumbean's Street" sign to the wall. Attach the children's houses along the street for a delightful display!

IGLOO

Materials: sugar cubes, ice blocks

Directions: Purchase two or three boxes of sugar cubes and ask the children to take turns building a sugar cube igloo. Read PERCY AND THE FIVE HOUSES by Else Holmelund Minarik to give them some guidelines for building; however, the children should feel free to create whatever they desire. Warn children not to eat the sugar cubes. Once they've been handled, they are dirty and should not be eaten. Those living in a cold climate can make a real igloo by freezing ice water in buckets and arranging the blocks into the shape of an igloo. Also, igloo kits containing forms for ice blocks are available and may be purchased in variety stores.

TEPEE

Materials: tepee pattern, toothpicks, glue, scissors, colored paper, markers, stapler

Directions: Use the pattern provided (enlarge it if you like) to cut out a tepee for each child. Let the children color the tepees with American Indian designs. Show the children how to cut on the dotted line and fold back the paper for an entrance. Overlap and staple the edges together to make a cone shape. Have the children dip toothpicks into glue and attach in the opening at the top.

Stand-up House Pattern

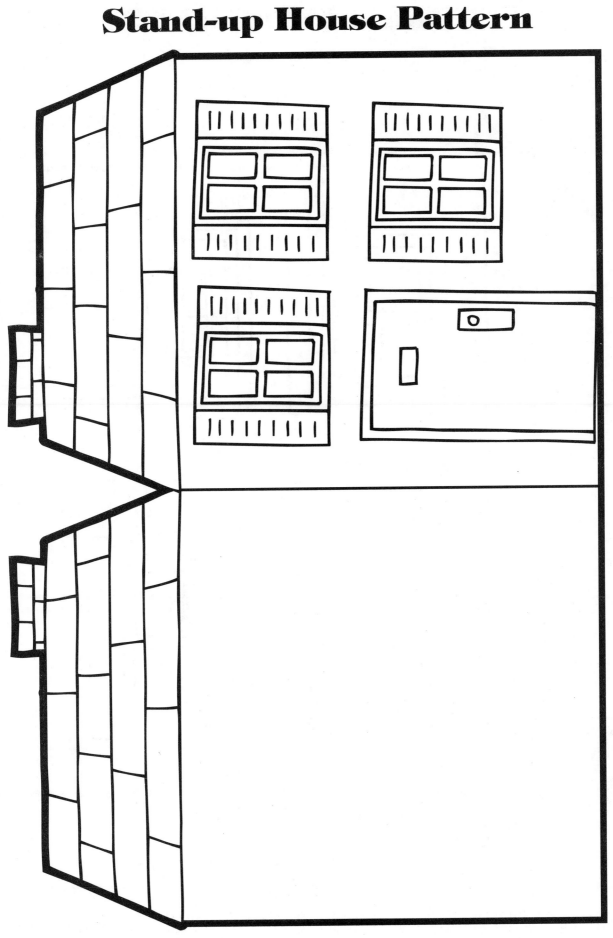

House Pattern

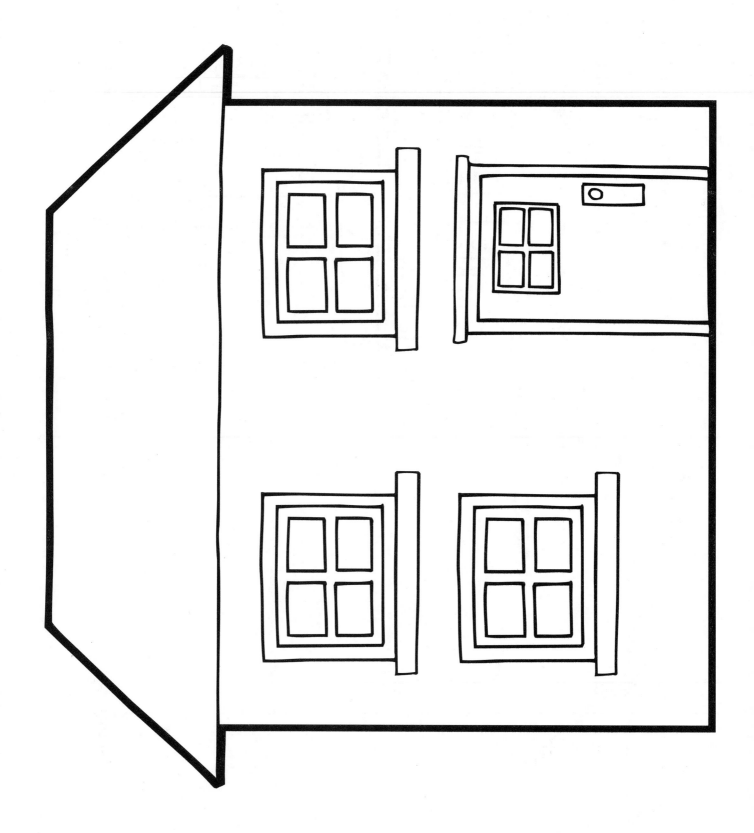

Tepee Pattern

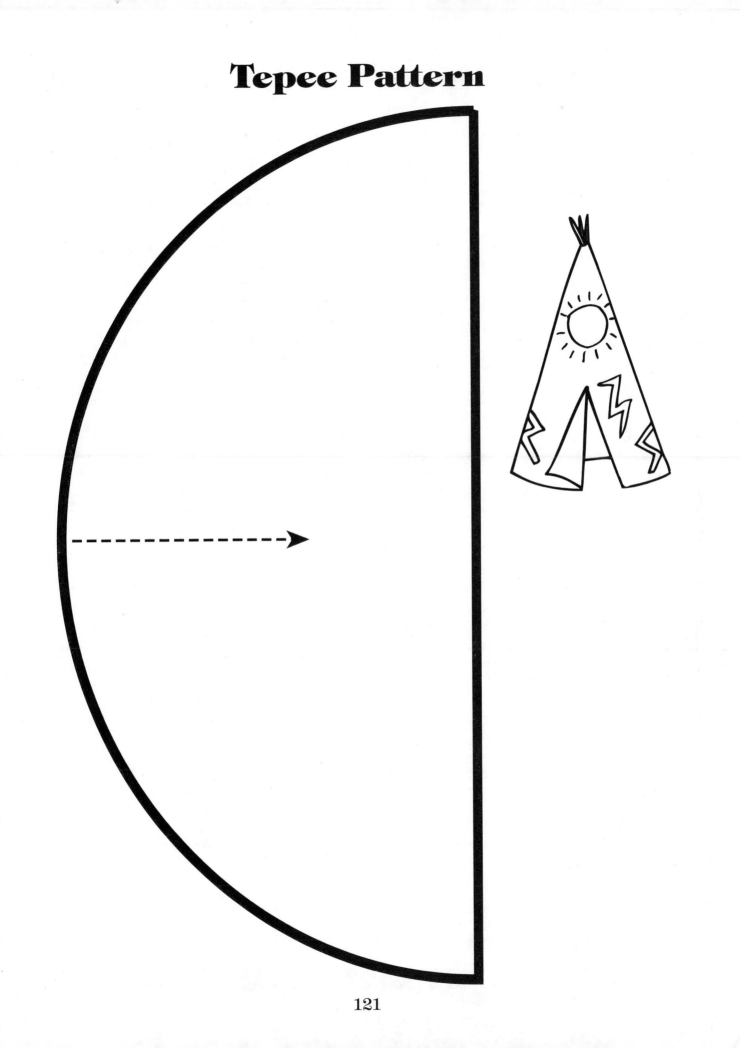

ORANGE SPLOT HOUSE COOKIES

Bake these cookies after reading THE BIG ORANGE SPLOT. Makes about 6 dozen cookies. Trace the house pattern onto poster paper before using.

3/4 cup margarine or butter
3/4 cup shortening
2 cups sugar
4 eggs
2 tsp. vanilla flavoring
5 cups flour
2 tsp. baking powder
1 tsp. salt
orange frosting

Combine butter, shortening, sugar, eggs, and vanilla and mix thoroughly. Mix the flour, baking powder, and salt together and blend in. Chill at least 2 hours. Heat the oven to 375 degrees. Roll the dough about 1/8" to 1/4" thick. Lay the house pattern on the dough and cut out; continue cutting out house-shaped cookies. Bake on an ungreased cookie sheet for 6 to 8 minutes. While the cookies are still warm, drip orange frosting onto the roof of the cookies to make the orange splot. Let the children do as much of the mixing, baking, and decorating as possible.

CRACKER HOUSE

The children will enjoy pretending to be Hansel and Gretel while munching on their graham cracker house!

5 whole graham crackers
stiff white frosting
assorted candies and cookies
(suggestions: small Tootsie Rolls for chimneys, round candies for roof, cookie for doors, and small gumdrops around the edge of the base)

Cover the work area with waxed paper. To make the base of each house, let the children frost two crackers on the long edges and stick together. Have them spread the entire base with frosting. Then have the children break the other three crackers in half and spread frosting along the edges of four of the halves. Help them stand these up on the frosted base, putting the frosted edges together to form the four walls; they may have to hold the crackers in place for a minute or two while the frosting sets. Tell the children to spread frosting along the edges of the two remaining half crackers and place them on the walls to form the roof. The children may frost the roof if desired, and decorate with candies and cookies.

BANANA IN A HOUSE

(serves 20)

10 hot dog buns
5 small bananas
peanut butter
jelly
raisins
peanuts
chocolate pieces

Spread peanut butter and jelly on the opened buns. Halve bananas lengthwise and place a half in each house (bun). Let the children sprinkle the sandwiches with peanuts, raisins, and chocolate pieces. Close each bun and cut in half crosswise.

RESOURCES

BOOKS

Bauer, Caroline Feller. **CELEBRATIONS** (H.W. Wilson, 1985).

Bauer, Caroline Feller. **HANDBOOK FOR STORYTELLERS** (American Library Assoc., 1977).

Bauer, Caroline Feller. **THIS WAY TO BOOKS** (H.W. Wilson, 1983).

Beall, Pamela Conn and Susan Hagen Nipp. **WEE SING** (Price/Stern/Sloan, 1982).

Beall, Pamela Conn and Susan Hagen Nipp. **WEE SING AND PLAY** (Price/Stern/Sloan, 1985).

Beall, Pamela Conn and Susan Hagen Nipp. **WEE SING SILLY SONGS** (Price/Stern/Sloan, 1983).

Catron, Carol Elaine and Barbara Catron Parks. **SUPER STORY TELLING** (T.S. Denison, 1986).

Courson, Diane, il. by Elizabeth Nygaard. **LET'S LEARN ABOUT FAIRY TALES AND NURSERY RHYMES** (Good Apple, 1988).

de Paola, Tomie. **TOMIE DE PAOLA'S MOTHER GOOSE** (Putnam, 1985).

Dowell, Ruth I., il. by Concetta C. Scott. **MOVE OVER, MOTHER GOOSE** (Gryphon House, 1987).

Evans, Joy and Jo Ellen Moore. **FUN WITH BOOKS** (Evan-Moor, 1987).

Evans, Joy and Jo Ellen Moore. **MORE FUN WITH BOOKS** (Evan-Moor, 1987).

Flint Public Library. **RING A RING O'ROSES: FINGER PLAYS FOR PRE-SCHOOL CHILDREN** (Flint Public Library, 1026 E. Kearsley St., Flint, MI 48502, 1988).

Glazer, Tom. **EYE WINKER, TOM TINKER, CHIN CHOPPER** (Doubleday, 1973).

Hearne, Betsy. **CHOOSING BOOKS FOR CHILDREN** (Delacorte, 1981).

Kimmel, Margaret Mary and Elizabeth Segel. **FOR READING OUT LOUD!** (Dell, 1983).

Landsberg, Michelle. **READING FOR THE LOVE OF IT** (Prentice-Hall, 1987).

Lima, Caroyln W. and John A. **A TO ZOO SUBJECT ACCESS TO CHILDREN'S PICTURE BOOKS** (R.R. Bowker, 1989).

Maquire, Jack. **CREATIVE STORYTELLING** (McGraw-Hill, 1985).

Oppenheim, Joanne, Barbara Brenner and Betty D. Boegehold. **CHOOSING BOOKS FOR KIDS** (Ballantine, 1986).

POEMS TO READ TO THE VERY YOUNG selected by Josette Frank, il. by Eloise Wilkin. (Random House, 1982).

Prelutsky, Jack, il. by James Stevenson. **THE NEW KID ON THE BLOCK** (Greenwillow, 1984).

Prelutsky, Jack, il. by Garth Williams. **RIDE A PURPLE PELICAN** (Greenwillow 1986).

THE RANDOM HOUSE BOOK OF POETRY FOR CHILDREN selected by Jack Prelutsky, il. by Marc Brown (Random House, 1983).

READ-ALOUD RHYMES FOR THE VERY YOUNG selected by Jack Prelutsky, il. by Marc Brown (Knopf, 1986).

Riggrers, Maxine. **AMAZING ALLIGATORS** (Monday Morning Books, 1990).

Silverstein, Shel. **A LIGHT IN THE ATTIC** (Harper & Row, 1981).

Silverstein, Shel. **WHERE THE SIDEWALK ENDS** (Harper & Row, 1974).

Sitarz, Paula Gaj. **PICTURE BOOK STORY HOURS** (Libraries Unlimited, 1987).

Trelease, Jim. **THE READ-ALOUD HANDBOOK** (Penguin, 1982).

Wendelin, Karla Hawkins, and M. Jean Greenlaw. **STORYBOOK CLASSROOMS** (Humanics, 1986).

White, Mary Lou, editor. **ADVENTURING WITH BOOKS** (National Council of Teachers of English, 1981).

PROPS

A Child's Collection, 155 Avenue of the Americas, New York, NY 10013

Creative Teaching Press, P.O. Box 6017, Cypress, CA 90630-0017

Folkmanis, Inc., 1219 Park Avenue, Emeryville, CA 94608

Peaceable Kingdom Press, 2954 Hillegass Avenue, Berkeley, CA 94705

Trudy Toy Company, Norwalk, KY

METRIC CONVERSION CHART:

Temperatures:
To convert Fahrenheit to Celsius, subtract 32 and multiply by 5/9.

205 F = 96.1 C
300 F = 148.8 C
325 F = 162.8 C
350 F = 177 C (baking)
375 F = 190.5 C
400 F = 204.4 C (hot oven)
425 F = 218.3 C
450 F = 232 C (very hot oven)

Capacity:
1/2 teaspoon = 2.5 ml.
1 teaspoon = 5 ml.
5 teaspoons = 25 ml.
1 tablespoon = 15 ml.
1/4 cup = 59.25 ml.
1/3 cup = 79 ml.
1/2 cup = 118.5 ml.
2/3 cup = 158 ml.
3/4 cup = 177.75 ml.
1 cup = 237 ml.
1 1/2 cups = 355.5 ml.

Weight:
1 ounce = 28.3 grams
7 ounces = 198.1 grams

Length:
1/8 inch = .3175 cm.
1/4 inch = .635 cm.
1 inch = 2.54 cm.
1 foot = 30.48 cm.

A

ALICE'S SPECIAL ROOM (111)
ANANSI AND THE MOSS-COVERED ROCK (8, 21)
ANIMALS SHOULD DEFINITELY NOT WEAR CLOTHING (31)
ANNA BANANA AND ME (50)
ANNA'S SECRET FRIEND (50)
ANT AND THE ELEPHANT, THE (8)
ANT CITIES (13)
ANTS CAN'T DANCE (9, 18)
ANTS DON'T GET SUNDAY OFF (15)
ARANEA: A STORY ABOUT A SPIDER (5, 15)
ARGYLE (34)

B

BE NICE TO SPIDERS (13)
BENEATH A BLUE UMBRELLA (16)
BENEDICT FINDS A HOME (111)
BENJY AND HIS FRIEND FIFI (54)
BENNY BAKES A CAKE (76)
BENTLY & EGG (57)
BEST BUG TO BE, THE (13)
BEST FRIENDS (selected by Lee Bennett Hopkins— 58)
BEST FRIENDS (by Steven Kellogg—55)
BEST FRIENDS CLUB, THE (57)
BEST FRIENDS FOR FRANCES (55)
BEST PRESENT, THE (91)
BIG BLOCK OF CHOCOLATE, THE (76)
BIG FAT WORM, THE (15)
BIG ORANGE SPLOT, THE (106, 117, 122)
BIG SHOE, LITTLE SHOE (31)
BIGGEST HOUSE IN THE WORLD, THE (106)
BLUEBERRIES FOR SAL (75, 80)
BOY HAD A MOTHER WHO BOUGHT HIM A HAT, A (33)
BREAD AND JAM FOR FRANCES (69)
BUGS (14)
BUNNIES AND THEIR GRANDMA (90)

C

CAKE FOR BARNEY, A (73)
CAKE THAT MACK ATE, THE (69)
CAPS FOR SALE (25, 34)
CAT IN THE HAT, THE (34)
CATERPILLAR AND THE POLLIWOG, THE (14)
CHARLIE NEEDS A CLOAK (31)
CHICKEN SUNDAY (56)
CLOUDY WITH A CHANCE OF MEATBALLS (67, 70, 81)
COCO CAN'T WAIT (85, 95, 97)
COME A TIDE (91)
COME OVER TO MY HOUSE (112)
COME TO THE MEADOW (90)
COULD BE WORSE (93)
CREEPY CRAWLY CRITTER RIDDLES (16)

D

DADDY HAS A PAIR OF STRIPED SHORTS (33)
DANDELION (32)
DAY WITH WILBUR ROBINSON, A (91)
DIAL-A-CROC (54)
DO YOUR EARS HANG LOW? (59)
DON'T FORGET THE BACON (74)
DOORBELL RANG, THE (70)
DRESS I'LL WEAR TO THE PRESS, THE (33)
DUNCAN & DOLORES (56)

E

EENCY WEENCY SPIDER (14)
ELMER BLUNT'S OPEN HOUSE (112)
EMPEROR'S NEW CLOTHES, THE (31)
EYE WINKER, TOM TINKER, CHIN CHOPPER (36)

F

FARMER IN THE SOUP, THE (75)
FEEL BETTER, ERNEST (57)
FIREFLIES! (13)
FIREFLIES IN THE NIGHT (13)
500 HATS OF BARTHOLOMEW CUBBINS, THE (25, 34)
FLY AWAY HOME (110)
FLYING SHOES, THE (33)
FOR LAUGHING OUT LOUD (16, 94)
FOX AND HEGGIE (51, 61)
FRIEND FOR OSCAR MOUSE, A (55)
FRIEND LIKE YOU, A (56)
FRIENDS (54)
FROG, DUCK AND RABBIT (54)
FROGGY GETS DRESSED (33)

G

GEORGE AND MARTHA ROUND AND ROUND (55)
GIANT JAM SANDWICH, THE (14, 75)
GRAMMY'S HOUSE (112)
GRANDADDY'S PLACE (90)
GRANDFATHER TANG'S STORY (85, 96)
GRANDFATHER'S CAKE (92, 102)
GRANDMA, FELIX, AND MUSTAPHA BISCUIT (89)
GRANDMA MIX-UP, THE (92)
GRANDMA REMEMBERS (93)
GRANDMA'S PROMISE (92)
GRANDMA'S SECRET LETTER (89, 102)
GRANDMA'S WHEELCHAIR (90)
GRANDMOTHER'S CHAIR (92)
GRANDPA (89)
GRANDPA DAYS, THE (89)
GRANDPAPPY (89)
GRANDPA'S FACE (90)
GRANDPA'S GARDEN LUNCH (89)
GRANDPA'S SLIPPERS (86, 96)
GRANDPA'S SONG (91)
GRASSHOPPER ON THE ROAD (14)
GREEN EGGS AND HAM (76)
GREGORY THE TERRIBLE EATER (76)
GRETCHEN'S GRANDMA (92)
GROUCHY LADYBUG, THE (13)
GROWING VEGETABLE SOUP (73)
GROWN-UP TRAP, THE (56)

H

HANK AND FRANK FIX UP THE HOUSE (110)
HAPPY BIRTHDAY, SAM (83, 90)
HELLO, CAT YOU NEED A HAT (32)
HELLO HOUSE (111, 117)
HENRY'S AWFUL MISTAKE (15)
HO FOR A HAT! (27)
HOME PLACE (111)
HOORAY FOR SNAIL! (15)
HOT FUDGE (74)
HOUSE FOR HERMIT CRAB, A (110)
HOUSE IN TOWN, A (112)
HOUSE IS A HOUSE FOR ME, A (103, 111)
HOUSE THAT JACK BUILT, THE (111)
HOW JOE BEAR AND SAM THE MOUSE GOT
    TOGETHER (51)
HOW MANY BUGS IN A BOX? (13)

I

"I CAN'T" SAID THE ANT (9)
I GO WITH MY FAMILY TO GRANDMA'S (91)
I HAVE A FRIEND (52)
I KNOW A LADY (57)
I LIKE CATERPILLARS (13)
I LOVE SPIDERS (14)
I UNPACKED MY GRANDMOTHER'S TRUNK (95)
ICE CREAM SOUP (75)
IF AT FIRST YOU DO NOT SEE (13)
IF I WERE A CRICKET (14)
IF YOU GIVE A MOOSE A MUFFIN (75)
IF YOU GIVE A MOUSE A COOKIE (103)
I'M NOT OSCAR'S FRIEND ANYMORE (57)
IN A PEOPLE HOUSE (112)
IN MY TREEHOUSE (113)
IN OUR HOUSE (113)
IN THE NIGHT KITCHEN (76)
IS ANYONE HOME? (112)
IS THIS A HOUSE FOR HERMIT CRAB? (107)

J

JAKE BAKED THE CAKE (74)
JAM DAY (74)
JAMBERRY (73)
JENNIE'S HAT (27)
JESSE BEAR, WHAT WILL YOU WEAR? (28)
JESSICA (54)
JONATHAN MOUSE AND THE BABY BIRD (56)
JUST MY FRIEND AND ME (55)
JUST MY SIZE (32)

K

KEEPING HOUSE (112)
KEVIN'S GRANDMA (93)
KNOTS ON A COUNTING ROPE (92)

L

LADY AND THE SPIDER, THE (14)
LADY WHO PUT SALT IN HER COFFEE, THE (74)
LEO THE LION (57)
LET'S BE FRIENDS AGAIN! (57)
LET'S EAT (74)

LET'S FIND OUT ABOUT HOUSES (113)
LITTLE BEAR'S TROUSERS (32)
LITTLE BUG (13)
LITTLE HOUSE OF YOUR OWN, A (111)
LITTLE HOUSE, THE (110)
LITTLE MOUSE'S PAINTING (57)
LITTLE POLAR BEAR (54)
LOOP THE LOOP (54)
LOUISE BUILDS A HOUSE (107)

M

MAGIC HOUSE, THE (111)
MAID AND THE MOUSE AND THE ODD-SHAPED
    HOUSE, THE(113)
MAN AND HIS HAT, A (34)
MANDY (89)
MARIANNA MAY AND NURSEY (31)
MARTIN'S HATS (28)
MARY WORE HER RED DRESS AND HENRY WORE
    HIS GREEN SNEAKERS (29, 38)
MAY I BRING A FRIEND? (52, 60)
MICE WHO LIVED IN A SHOE, THE (112)
MILLICENT AND THE WIND (56)
MISSING TARTS, THE (74)
MONSTER AND THE TAILOR, THE (29, 39)
MOON, STARS, FROGS AND FRIENDS (55)
MORE SPAGHETTI, I SAY! (73)
MOUSE IN MY HOUSE, A (113)
MOUSEKIN FINDS A FRIEND (56)
MOUSEKIN'S GOLDEN HOUSE (108)
MOVE OVER, MOTHER GOOSE (36, 78)
MY FRIEND THE MOON (53)
MY GRANDMOTHER'S COOKIE JAR (92)
MY GREAT GRANDPA (93)
MY POPPA LOVES OLD MOVIES (90)

N

NAPPING HOUSE, THE (103, 113)
NATIONAL WORM DAY (15)
NATTIE PARSON'S GOOD-LUCK LAMB (31)
NETTIE JO'S FRIENDS (56)
NEW HOUSE FOR LITTLE MOUSE, A (113)
NEW TREASURY OF CHILDREN'S POETRY, A (58)
NICHOLAS CRICKET (14)
NIGHT NOISES (86)
NO FRIENDS (57, 66)
NORA'S STARS (91)
NOT THE PIANO, MRS. MEDLEY (91)

O

OLD HOUSE, THE (110)
ON GRANDMA'S ROOF (93)
ONE THOUSAND POEMS FOR CHILDREN (16)
OSCAR MOUSE FINDS A HOME (108, 112)
OUR HOUSE ON THE HILL (111)

P

PATCHWORK QUILT, THE (90)
PERCY AND THE FIVE HOUSES (109, 118)
PHILHARMONIC GETS DRESSED, THE (33)
PIECE OF CAKE, A (75)
PIZZA MAN (75)
POCKET FOR CORDUROY, A (25, 32)
POPCORN (71)
POPCORN DRAGON, THE (71)
PORCUPINE NAMED FLUFFY, A (55)
POSSUM STEW (73)
POTATO MAN, THE (75)
PRINCIPAL'S NEW CLOTHES, THE (31)
PUMPKIN, PUMPKIN (72)
PUNKY SPENDS THE DAY (93)
PURPLE COAT, THE (32)

Q

QUANGLE WANGLE'S HAT, THE (25, 33)

R

RAG COAT, THE (30)
RANDOM HOUSE BOOK OF POETRY FOR
    CHILDREN, THE (94)
READ-ALOUD RHYMES FOR THE VERY YOUNG (16,
    35, 58)
READER'S DIGEST CHILDREN'S SONGBOOK (79,
    115)
RECHENKA'S EGGS (67, 76, 81)
RIDE A PURPLE PELICAN (25, 35, 94)
RING A RING O'ROSES (36, 58, 78)
ROSEBUD AND RED FLANNEL (30)
RUNAWAY MITTENS (34)

S

SHOES FROM GRANDPA (31)
SHOPPING BASKET, THE (73)
SING A SONG OF POPCORN (16, 114)
SNAIL'S SPELL, THE (15)
SOME OF MY BEST FRIENDS ARE MONSTERS (56)
SONG AND DANCE MAN (89)
STINGY BAKER, THE (74)
STONE SOUP (72)

T

TACKY THE PENGUIN (53, 62)
TAN TAN'S HAT (32)
TAN TAN'S SUSPENDERS (32)
THIS IS THE HAT: A STORY IN RHYME (34)
THIS IS THE PLACE FOR ME (109)
THREE FRIENDS, THE (55)
THREE HAT DAY, A (32)
THROUGH GRANDPA'S EYES (92)
THUNDER CAKE (76)
TONY'S BREAD (73)
TOO MANY BOOKS (110)
TROUBLE WITH GRAN, THE (87)
TROUBLE WITH GRANDAD, THE (89)
TROUBLE WITH TROLL (31)
TWO BAD ANTS (10)

U

UNCLE HAROLD AND THE GREEN HAT (32)

V

VERY BUSY SPIDER, THE (10)
VERY HUNGRY CATERPILLAR, THE (11)
VERY QUIET CRICKET, THE (11)
VERY SPECIAL HOUSE, A (112)

W

WALKING COAT, THE (34)
WALTER'S TAIL (54)
WATCH OUT FOR THE CHICKEN FEET IN YOUR
    SOUP (73)

WE LIKE BUGS (13)
WEDNESDAY SURPRISE, THE (89)
WEE SING (94, 115)
WHAT'S SO GREAT ABOUT CINDY SNAPPLEBY?
    (56)
WHEN I AM OLD WITH YOU (91)
WHEN I GO VISITING (87)
WHEN THE MOON SHINES BRIGHTLY ON THE
    HOUSE (110)
WHERE IS MY FRIEND? (55)
WHERE THE SIDEWALK ENDS (25, 35, 58, 114)
WHO IS COMING TO OUR HOUSE? (113)
WHO TOOK THE FARMER'S HAT? (33)
WHO'S IN RABBIT'S HOUSE? (110)
WHOSE SHOE? (33)
WHY MOSQUITOES BUZZ IN PEOPLE'S EARS (12)
WILLIAM AND GRANDPA (88, 102)
WIND IN THE WILLOWS: HOME SWEET HOME (110)
WITH LOVE FROM GRANDMA (93)
WOLF'S CHICKEN STEW, THE (74)
WOMAN WITH THE EGGS, THE (73)
WOMBAT STEW (76)
WOODEN DOLL, THE (88)
WORM'S TALE, A (12)

Y

YOUR OWL FRIEND (54)
YUMMERS! (75)